Substitute Teaching from A to Z

Substitute Teaching from A to Z

Barbara Pressman

New York   Chicago   San Francisco   Lisbon   London   Madrid   Mexico City
Milan   New Delhi   San Juan   Seoul   Singapore   Sydney   Toronto

Library of Congress Cataloging-in-Publication Data

Pressman, Barbara L.
    Substitute teaching from A to Z / Babara L. Pressman.
       p.   cm.
    Includes bibliographical references (p. 227–233) and index.
    ISBN 0-07-149632-7 (alk. paper)
      1. Substitute teaching—Handbooks, manuals, etc.   2. Substitute teachers—
Handbooks, manuals, etc.   I. Title.

   LB2844.1.S8P74   2007
   371.14'122—dc22   2007009865

   9 10 11 12 13 14 15 16 17 18 19 20 21 22   QFR/QFR   1 5 4 3

ISBN 978-0-07-149632-2
MHID   0-07-149632-7

Interior illustrations by Steve Springer

McGraw-Hill books are available at special quantity discounts to use as premiums and sales promotions or for use in corporate training programs. To contact a representative, please visit the Contact Us pages at www.mhprofessional.com.

This book is printed on acid-free paper.

To Roger, Matt, and Michael

Contents

Foreword

My youngest son is currently a high school senior, and, unlike his father at his age, the young man is a serious student. Yet, he has told me on more than one occasion, "Hey, when a sub shows up, I shut down. It's time to chill."

Sadly, his attitude about substitute teachers is similar to one expressed by a superintendent of schools who said, "I wish it were not the case, but substitute teachers are nothing more than glorified babysitters."

Too many people, students, and educators believe that when a sub appears at the door of a classroom, learning is rarely the outcome. And yet, each day across America substitute teachers take charge of an estimated 300,000 classrooms. In the thirteen years of a child's education, from Kindergarten to twelfth grade, a typical student will have had a substitute teacher for the equivalent of almost one full year!

These numbers provide a compelling argument that substitute teachers play a vital role in our educational landscape. They are an essential part of a child's education. Finding ways to improve the entire substitute teaching system is crucial to improving our schools and providing our children with the finest education possible.

It is indeed a pleasure to write the foreword to *Substitute Teaching from A to Z*. A practical, well-written book on this subject is long overdue and will fill a vital need in our efforts to improve the quality of substitute teachers.

Barbara Pressman is a veteran teacher who has been able to translate her classroom know-how and her experience in training new subs and student teachers into a book that presents "a true hands-on approach" and a "toolbox of ideas and resources" for subs. As you read *Substitute Teaching from A to Z*, you'll learn how to deal with difficult days and apply key survival strategies in the classroom. But you'll also learn teaching fundamentals such as questioning techniques and how to introduce yourself to your students. Barbara presents these valuable lessons along with real-life classroom vignettes to make the material accessible and enjoyable.

I have personally observed Barbara working with new substitute teachers and have seen her show them strategies to make them successful in a variety of settings. She has written a book that any substitute teacher—novice or veteran—can benefit from reading.

Substitute Teaching from A to Z will make you a better sub and, as a consequence, will add to the quality of the learning experience of children you teach each day.

Gregory F. Aloia, Ph.D.
Dean and Professor
Florida Atlantic University
College of Education

Preface

It's 6:30 A.M. You wake to the shrill ring of your telephone, answering quickly so you don't disturb the entire household. Groggy, you try to focus as the local sub coordinator asks, "Are you available for a Kindergarten classroom in Mary Tracy School?" There's a hint of desperation in the coordinator's voice.

You pause for just a moment, weighing the pros and cons of spending the day with a group of rambunctious five-year-olds. There's no doubt it will be a physically exhausting day. But you'll get to sing songs and read stories. You might even come home with pictures of rainbows and butterflies, made with love—just for you!

"I'll take it!" you say.

And so, your day as a substitute teacher begins.

Substitute teaching is always challenging because you never know what to expect. One day, you might encounter a difficult class that fills your day with frustration. But on other days, you and the children will really "click." You'll feel the joy that only a good teacher can feel as real learning happens.

Every day, you'll have an opportunity to reach out and touch a child that needs a little TLC. You might even have an opportunity to truly make a difference in a child's life. There will be smiles and frowns, laughter and tears, and numerous pictures to hang on your refrigerator. It's all in a day's work for a substitute teacher.

I have written Substitute Teaching from A to Z to help you become an effective substitute teacher. The book has been designed to provide you with useful guidance in a reader-friendly format. Each chapter corresponds to one letter of the alphabet, addressing a vital topic that will help you to be a better teacher and a more effective sub.

Substitute Teaching from A to Z presents a true hands-on approach and provides a toolbox of ideas and resources that will help you solve subbing problems. In my experience, theory provides very little help when you walk into another teacher's classroom. What you need is pragmatic guidance, and that's what you'll get with this book. Each chapter begins with an anecdote based on actual events from my own experience and the experience of colleagues and friends. (I've changed the names of teachers and students and the locations and names of all schools to protect the privacy of those involved.) The anecdotes set the stage for step-by-step suggestions, helpful hints, and proven ideas that will make your classroom experience more rewarding (and easier!). I've also created a website—**substituteteachingatoz.com**—where you'll find many pointers to valuable resources—some in print and others available on the Web.

Take the suggestions, hints, and ideas presented in *Substitute Teaching from A to Z* and make them your own. Refer to this book often, after a good day or a difficult one. Highlight the suggestions that you feel will be most helpful for your needs. Keep a folder of helpful suggestions that have worked for others and for you.

As a substitute teacher, you belong to a select group of people. You are a capable, organized, intelligent, brave, and caring human being. Hold your head high and start your day with confidence. The rewards will be worth it!

Acknowledgments

The wonderful thing about teaching is that it enables you to continue learning. I want to thank the people who have enabled me to follow the path of teaching and learning throughout my life.

My first teachers were my parents, Alvin and Hannah Laster. Their loving example and gentle guidance gave me the confidence to pursue my goals. My brother, Ken, and sisters, Diana and Laura (who lost her struggle against cancer five years ago), have been a constant source of love and friendship in my life.

My sons, Matt and Michael, have been my most important "students." You learned well and have made me very proud, but you've also taught me very important life lessons. You are my joy.

I have been a teacher for many years and have had an opportunity to influence the lives of students ranging from kindergarteners to college seniors. Nothing has been more rewarding. To the many, many children I taught in Orange, Connecticut, you enriched my life. I remember every one of you! To my students at Florida Atlantic University, I gained so much knowledge from watching you grow to be fine educators.

Thank you to my editor, Kathryn Keil at McGraw-Hill, for believing in this project and recognizing the need for a book to improve the quality of substitute teachers.

Most of all, I want to thank my husband, Roger Pressman. He has been listening to my "teacher stories" for more than thirty years and was the first person to encourage me to write a book about my experiences in the classroom. He has been my loving partner and has guided me through this project. I couldn't have written this book without him! My thanks always for his love and support.

How to Use This Book

When I decided to write *Substitute Teaching from A to Z*, I wanted to create a readable and informative guide for practicing substitute teachers and for those people who are considering giving substitute teaching a try. Although I had many goals as I began writing, my primary intent was to provide you with the teaching tools you'll need to walk into any classroom with confidence.

Throughout this book, I'll try to show you how to manage a classroom of students with kindness and control. I'll present real-life lessons that I have learned through many years of classroom teaching and translate these into useful guidelines that you can apply daily as you teach. I'll avoid education theory and instead emphasize proven, pragmatic advice that applies whether you're subbing in Kindergarten or middle school.

Not everyone is a born teacher. But you can learn to teach—if your heart is in the right place and you're willing to learn from the successes and failures of those who have preceded you. *Substitute Teaching from A to Z* distills lessons learned and provides you with useful guidance as you work to improve your teaching skills.

Who should read this book?

You're someone who is thinking about becoming a sub. Maybe you're a college graduate (with an education degree) and have a few months before starting a full-time teaching job. Possibly you're a recent grad in some other discipline who hasn't yet landed a job and wants to give subbing a try. You might be a mom or dad who is interested in a job that coincides with your child's school schedule. Maybe you're a retiree who has always wanted to teach but never had the opportunity. *Substitute Teaching from A to Z* is for you.

You're a rookie (beginning) substitute teacher. You've filled out the applications, passed your background check, and may have had a few subbing assignments. But you're still a rookie. You need guidance on a broad range of issues that every sub will face, and you don't have a lot of time to learn them! *Substitute Teaching from A to Z* is for you.

You're a seasoned substitute teacher. You've weathered the classroom "wars" and survived them unscathed. Although you do well most of the time, you continue to struggle with certain classes. As a good teacher, you recognize that there's always more to learn and many ways to hone your craft. *Substitute Teaching from A to Z* is for you.

How should I use this book?

Every chapter in this book addresses an important topic for substitute teachers. Each chapter has been designed to stand on its own. Therefore, you need not read the book from front to back (although it certainly wouldn't hurt to do so!).

My advice is to scan the table of contents from A to Z. Pick one or more topics that represent immediate challenges—things you need to know in order to approach tomorrow's assignment with confidence. Then, read those chapters. As time passes, you'll find that other challenges will present themselves and other chapters will become important to you.

Each chapter begins with a real-life anecdote drawn from my own experience and the experience of colleagues, friends, and other substitute teachers. It sets the tone for the chapter and provides its own built-in message. I urge you to take the time to read each one.

The chapter content is organized in a question-and-answer format. The questions that I've presented are those that new teachers often ask their mentors—if they're lucky enough to have one. I've tried to keep every answer short and to the point, but more important, I've tried to provide real-world guidance that you can use immediately. Finally, every chapter contains a summary that distills the most important guidelines into a series of bulleted points. Be sure to read it.

What's the best way to use the Dear Barbara letters?

Each Dear Barbara letter addresses a particular concern or problem that all subs face in their daily relationships with colleagues and students. One letter—formatted as a sidebar—is presented in each chapter.

The content of each letter is independent of the chapter content and is intended to help you tackle issues that may come up while subbing at all grade levels. The letters address topics such as:

- A paraprofessional who is not helpful
- Angry parents
- Students with negative behaviors
- Mental health problems
- Full-time job opportunities
- Taking the class to an assembly
- Alternatives to yelling
- First impressions

These letters are great to read *before* an incident occurs and will serve to guide your actions as you run across similar problems in your own experience. I invite you to pose your own Dear Barbara question, and I would be happy to answer it. Go to my website, **substituteteachingatoz.com**, and post your question or concern. My answer will appear online. Your experiences and insights are important to me and to my readers. I've created **substituteteachingatoz.com** to provide you with a portal to additional resources and links that will help you become a better substitute teacher. These resources will be updated as new sources of information on substitute teaching appear in print and on the Web.

A year from now, your copy of Substitute Teaching from A to Z may be dog-eared and scruffy, but I hope that it will continue to be an important resource for you as you advance in your subbing experience. Enjoy the book!

Introduction

The last month had been hard on Jessica Martinez. A college graduate with a degree in English, she had been "downsized" out of a job with a major ad agency and she was adrift. Jessica and her friend Liza were sitting at the kitchen table in the apartment they shared.

"You know, maybe I should do what you do," said Jessica.

Liza looked shocked. "You mean . . . you want to be a teacher?"

"I've always liked children, and, well, I could go back to school and . . ."

"That would be awesome!" said Liza. "But how are you going to pay the rent?"

"I was thinking I could substitute teach for a while. See if I like it. Make some money while I take courses, you know."

Liza smiled. "Subbing? You know it's not so easy."

Jessica paused and then looked into her friend's eyes. "Yeah, but you can help me learn the basics, can't you?"

Liza smiled again. "It'll be an adventure, but at least we'll be able to share teacher stories."

I have no doubt that Liza, a certified classroom teacher, could help Jessica overcome the initial obstacles that every new teacher must navigate. But what if you don't have a good friend who's a classroom teacher? What if the teacher acquaintances you do have simply don't have the time or the inclination to help? I suppose that's why you're reading this book.

Before we get started with *Substitute Teaching from A to Z*, it's worth considering a few introductory questions that will set the stage for the chapters that follow.

Why should I become a substitute teacher?

The answer to this question depends on your situation. If you've always thought about becoming a teacher but have never been in front of two dozen or so children, it's a good way to test the waters. If you're actively looking for a teaching job, subbing is one of the best ways to obtain a permanent position. It can also be a wonderful way to learn your craft. If you're in a transitional period in your life and want to make a few dollars while at the same time establishing a lifestyle in which you have the freedom to make your own schedule, subbing may be right for you.

But remember, if you walk into the classroom without the necessary tools, subbing can be a nightmare. Your best-laid plans for a future in teaching will evaporate, and your desire to teach may disappear. And that would be a shame because you can master subbing. It's just that you may need some help. You'll need to be confident, prepared, and ready for the challenge. *Substitute Teaching from A to Z* can serve as your personal mentor.

Can subbing lead to a full-time teaching position?

It certainly can. That's how I got my teaching job. Subbing is your "audition" at each school you visit. Once school administrators get to know you and your talents, you can become a candidate for a potential teaching position. You're a known commodity. You have proven that you can fit into the faculty, and it's very clear that you are a team player. The children and parents have responded warmly to you. Why hire a perfect stranger when you're already on board?

Of course, it's important to remember that every school district board has a set of requirements for full-time teachers that may be different from those for subs. You'll have to meet all full-time requirements before you'll be able to apply for a full-time position.

How do I fit in at the school?

You are vital part of the faculty. Remember that a school cannot survive without subs. If a sub is not available on a given day, one of the specialists (e.g., the art teacher or the reading specialist) may have to take over a classroom. There are even times when the principal may have to take over a first-grade class.

When this happens, no one on the faculty is happy. Why? Because specialists provide relief to classroom teachers and without them, teachers get no relief. For example, if the physical education teacher is asked to fill in for a classroom teacher because no sub is available, there will be no gym for all of the students that day. As a consequence, classroom teachers don't get the planning period they expect when their students were supposed to go to gym. Frowns all around! When *you* walk in, everyone breathes a sigh of relief.

How do I get on the sub list?

The larger the school system, the more red tape you'll encounter as you work to have your name placed on the list. Call the School Board office or go online to find out how to apply. Be sure to have an updated résumé available. Many communities require fingerprinting and a security clearance, which may take weeks. So plan to take care of the paperwork early and be prepared to wait.

Smaller school systems ask you to fill out a standard form and to provide references. Subs are needed so desperately that you may be working in no time! You should read any information given to you about rules and regulations of the particular school system and be prepared to abide by them.

Should I sub at just one school or many different schools?

Ideally, you should try to sub in a limited number of schools. After you have taken a few assignments at the schools, you'll become a known commodity. You'll begin to meet faculty members and become comfortable as part of the faculty. The students will get to know you and respect you, if they see you on a regular basis. You'll be familiar with school culture and routine.

Some subs are happiest at only one or two schools. They try to develop a relationship with administrators and teachers so that they will be requested explicitly when a sub is needed.

Of course, for maximum economic opportunity, the more schools, the better your weekly paycheck! But be careful of spreading yourself too thin.

How does the school system let me know if they need me?

Most larger school systems have an automated phone system, often called a Sub Locator. You will hear a taped message that describes an available sub opening. You are then asked to push a button indicating whether or not you have interest in the opening. You will be informed of your assignment, and your day begins. It's always a relief if you are notified a day ahead of time. You'll have more time to prepare and bring the proper materials with you.

Try to find out the methods used in your school system and learn the routine as early as possible. You'll avoid unnecessary stress.

Should I take every assignment that is offered?

If you are too choosy about which assignments you take, you will not be called very often. The sub coordinator does not want to waste time calling someone who will say no, and some automated systems prioritize their calling list based on the frequency with which a sub says yes to assignments that are offered. You are a tremendous asset to the school system if you say yes as often as possible. Reliability is a valued asset.

What about different subject areas? Should I teach all of them?

The advantage to subbing in all subject areas is that you will get to know all the students very quickly. For example, if you accept a PE position for a day, you may see half of all students in the school. On another day, when the students see you in their own classroom they will remember you. Familiarity and respect have already been established. They know that you truly are a "real" teacher. Your life is easier.

Another advantage to subbing in many classrooms and special areas is that you are exposed to many ways of handling situations. You might see something in the Resource Room that you have never seen in any other classroom. As you gather these ideas, you will become a much better teacher.

If you're willing to be flexible, you will be appreciated by faculty and administrators alike. You'll be rewarded with a continuing flow of subbing work and better assignments in the future.

Attendance and
the Morning Routine

I t was my very first day as a substitute teacher, and as I walked into my first assignment, a first-grade classroom at Greenhaven Elementary, I thought, "These are little children. What possible problems could I have?"

As it turned out . . . plenty! The lesson plans left for me were voluminous, with more detail than any human could ever need. "Morning meeting" consisted of the Pledge of Allegiance, a patriotic song, attendance, calendar activities, counting how many days the children had been in school, daily oral language, and on and on.

We began our day by saying the Pledge of Allegiance—a logical first step. As we began singing "You're a Grand Old Flag," I noticed little Michael in the back of the room, sobbing uncontrollably. As soon as I had a free minute, I walked to his desk and I asked him what was wrong.

"Miss Watson [the regular classroom teacher] always takes the attendance *before* the pledge," he sniffled. "You did everything out of order," he accused, as a tear rolled down his cheek.

I could see a few other children holding back tears in sympathy for their classmate.

From this experience, I learned very quickly how important routine is for younger children. A change in routine immediately increases classroom instability, and instability is not what a sub wants early in the day.

If you decide to modify the morning routine, tell the children that you will try to do things the right way, but sometimes you may change things "just a little." Ask them if that is okay and solicit their help in teaching you the normal procedure. They may feel a bit uneasy, but your request for help will make them feel like "big shots." Before long, smiles will begin to appear and the whole class will be on your side! You're working together as a team.

What's the best way to take attendance?

Taking attendance can be a real struggle because you don't know the students' names, and it is your very first opportunity to look incompetent. The teacher's plans should tell you how attendance is accomplished in this classroom, but often you're given no guidance. If your school uses attendance folders or notebooks, they will likely be on the teacher's desk or in the teacher's mailbox, in or near the school office.

The best way to be sure you get it right is to ask a *special helper* to assist you with this task. (See the Helpers chapter.) Choose a child who seems to be quiet and well-behaved. He or she can actually take attendance for you as the children arrive or just tell you who is absent. I have found this to be the most effective method when you don't know the names of the children.

If you decide to call out each child's name, be careful. If you mispronounce a name, it can be potentially disruptive, causing laughter and embarrassment for you and the student. If you have any doubt, ask the student (addressing him or her using the first name and last initial) to clarify the proper pronunciation.

Lunch count is usually part of the morning routine. Be sure to have your special helper do this record keeping as well.

Many school systems have gone to computerized record keeping. Check with office staff or with a grade-level partner in order to be consistent when performing computerized record keeping for attendance.

If you're subbing in a middle school or high school, attendance is taken in the homeroom before students proceed to their first period classes. In this situation, simply polling the students by name is all that is required. Alternatively, you can ask one responsible student to tell you who is absent that day.

When should I introduce myself?

Immediately after you take attendance, introduce yourself. The way you do this is very important and can make or break your day. In fact, it's so important I've dedicated an entire chapter, Introducing Yourself, to the subject.

How should I manage the morning routine?

I believe that the success of your day as a substitute teacher begins the minute you walk into the classroom. The success with which you manage the classroom morning routine will have much to do with the success of your day as a whole. In primary grades, the morning routine typically encompasses attendance and lunch count, the morning meeting, calendar activities, before-school work, a journal entry, and a problem of the day. Be sure that the students complete these before other school tasks.

By making yourself aware of the morning routine, you set the tone for the day—that this is a normal school day and that

When should I allow a student to visit the nurse?

Dear Barbara,

Last week, I was assigned to a first-grade classroom. The students were well behaved and cooperative for most of the day. But as soon as I announced that we would be starting math at 11:00, a steady stream of children asked to go to the nurse. It was obvious to me that this was an "avoidance" tactic.

I don't want to deny a sick child a visit for medical help, yet I am almost positive some faking was going on! I'm not sure how to handle it. What should I do?

Janina in Florida

Dear Janina,

Visits to the nurse are a common occurrence when you're subbing in the primary grades. Especially when you begin a subject that presents a challenge to younger children. Math is hard and even intimidating for some students, and what better way to avoid frustration and failure than going to the nurse?

Remember, the nurse is a nurturer. She shows sympathy, and she gives the children Band-Aids. She may even call Mom or Dad and let someone go home early!

Experienced teachers and subs are aware of the "nurse" tactic. Rather than embarrass a child or risk misreading a serious illness, I suggest that you tell the child that if she visits the nurse, she must be pretty sick, which means no recess. During recess, that child will have to sit near you. She won't be able to play with her classmates because sick children must rest as much as possible.

This response often brings on a miraculous recovery, and the visit to the nurse may be unnecessary after all!

normal work and work habits apply. As a consequence, your day will flow more smoothly.

How should I handle extraordinary events, such as fire drills?

There are events that occur during the day that are not part of the normal routine. Among the most common are fire drills, student assemblies, and special dismissals.

Try to familiarize yourself with fire-drill procedures. The students should be able to tell you where they usually exit, but it is important to be sure about this procedure. Fire-drill exit information should be posted somewhere in the room or included in a substitute folder. If not, the teacher next door will help you. *Always* bring a class list with you when you exit the school for a fire drill. This will allow you to determine whether any students are missing.

A special assembly is a welcome diversion during the school day. An announcement will be made on the public address system, and you'll have to line up your class. It's a good idea to follow the lead of the neighboring teacher. When you arrive at the auditorium, ask the students where they usually sit. After the program, classes normally return to their rooms in a predefined sequence. Try to determine when it's your turn to leave.

Once you've returned, you have a wonderful opportunity for discussion and possibly a quick lesson as a follow-up to the program. In the primary grades, you can ask the children to draw pictures and write about their favorite parts of the program. They can write thank-you notes to the presenter. Students in upper grades can write essays on the content or what part of the assembly was the most interesting to them. They can do some research on the subject in the computer lab. Use the assembly as a springboard for further learning.

It's likely that the assembly will create minor scheduling problems for you. You'll have to adjust the time line for the remainder of the day to ensure that you get most of the assigned work accomplished. If this cannot be done, be sure to include a comment about the assembly in your teacher note.

Sometimes, after an assembly, parents want to take their children home. In order to protect the students and to avoid being ensnared in a legal action, schools have very strict procedures that must be followed when a parent arrives to take a child home early. Clearance from the office is crucial for any early dismissal. Do not allow a parent to walk into your classroom and tell you he or she is taking the child to the dentist. Permission *must* be obtained from the school office. When in doubt, call the office for clearance. *Never* dismiss a child without approval from someone in the administration.

Summary

Proper handling of the morning routine can make or break your day as a sub. Be sure you follow these guidelines:

- When you arrive at school, stop in the office and find the mailbox of the teacher that you will be subbing for that day. It's likely that an attendance folder or notebook is in the mailbox. Bring it and other mail to the teacher's desk.
- Be sure to follow the morning routine as closely as possible, particularly in primary grades. This gives the students a feeling of stability and sets the tone for the rest of the day.
- Find a special helper to work with you on the attendance. Ask your helper to write down the names of the absent students on a separate piece of paper or tell you who is absent. If your helper cannot do this, find another child. Usually your instinct will guide you in making the correct choice. Then transfer the information into the attendance

book yourself. Upper grades are more self-sufficient, and a
trusted helper can take the attendance for you.
• Prepare for extraordinary events (e.g., fire drills) before
they happen. Be sure you know the procedure to follow.

I've found that it's difficult to recover from a bad start when
you're a sub. That's why the morning routine is so important.
Learn to perform it well, and your subbing day will go more
smoothly.

Bag of Tricks

Carmen Morales is always prepared. When students see her walk into their classroom, they relax, knowing that this substitute teacher will be in control and ready to spend a productive day with them. There will be no chaos when Mrs. Morales is in charge.

Carmen keeps her "bag of tricks" packed with teaching essentials and brings it to school each day. The bag contains items that might be useful for any circumstance that she is likely to encounter.

"Are we ready for today's spelling test?" asks Mrs. Morales in her trademark lilting voice.

A hand shoots into the air, attached to a little boy with a growing frown.

"Mrs. Morales, I can't take the spelling test. I don't have a pencil." The little boy seems close to tears.

Carmen smiles in a way that shows mild disapproval (after all, the student should have a pencil) but at the same time expresses sympathy. She reaches into her bag of tricks and out comes a well-sharpened pencil.

Later in the day after recess, a student named Lily reenters the classroom with a smudge of dirt on her face. Mrs. Morales takes out a hand wipe and quietly hands it to her, maintaining her privacy and saving her from embarrassment.

Lily's eyes widen as she wipes her face. "Wow, you have everything in there, Mrs. Morales!"

There's a reason that the Boy Scouts adopted the motto "Be Prepared." For a substitute teacher, nothing could be more important. In this chapter, I'll discuss some of the items that should be placed in your personal "bag of tricks."

Why should I bother with a bag of tricks?

It's a reasonable question. After all, the classroom is full of educational materials, there will be a complete daily schedule and plan that will guide you through every minute of the day, the children will always know where things are kept, and if they don't, a grade partner surely will. Right?

Think again. In too many cases, I've found that the right teaching materials may be missing or incomplete, the lesson plan is sketchy, the children don't know where things are kept, and the teacher next door can't provide much help. That's where your bag of tricks comes into play, and that's why you need one.

What should I pack in my bag of tricks?

Look at your bag of tricks as a portable mini-classroom. It should contain everything you'll need to make it through the day when classroom materials are less than adequate and you're left with open time after the lesson plan has been completed. Your bag of tricks should contain:

- Storybooks appropriate for three different grade levels (one or two really good short stories or a short age-appropriate mystery story for older grades)
- A book of funny poems
- Stickers and other rewards
- A whistle (for those PE and recess days)
- Worksheets for all levels
- A how-to-draw book
- A collection of reliable games and brainteasers (See the Games chapter.)
- Assorted school supplies (e.g., markers, crayons, pencils, notebook paper)
- Personal items for your use during the day

The Web Resources chapter contains many additional suggestions for materials that can be used for your bag of tricks. Browse the suggested websites (pointers can be found at **substituteteachingatoz.com**) and find a few worksheets that will be both fun and educational for a broad range of grade levels. Hundreds of websites provide brainteasers, math puzzles, word finds, and hidden pictures that can be used as a reward when students finish their work or as time fillers when class work is completed early.

As you gain experience as a sub, you'll collect many items for your bag. You may alternate these items depending on the grade level, the disposition of your students, and the available time. If you see a wonderful activity or set of materials that is being used by the classroom teacher, make yourself a copy so that you can use it in the future.

Can you suggest specific books for the bag of tricks?

Here are some favorites that have worked well for me. This list includes books for many different age levels and interests:

- *Alexander and the Terrible, Horrible, No Good, Very Bad Day* by Judith Viorst
- The *Arthur* series by Marc Brown

- *Chicken Soup for the Pet Lover's Soul* by Jack Canfield
- *Chicken Soup for the Teenage Soul* by Jack Canfield
- *Doctor De Soto* by William Steig
- *Encyclopedia Brown* by Donald J. Sobol
- *The Giving Tree* by Shel Silverstein
- *Great-Uncle Dracula* by Bonnie Bader
- *The Keeping Quilt* by Patricia Polacco
- *Miss Nelson Is Missing!* by Harry Allard and James Marshall
- *Pinkerton, Behave!* by Steven Kellogg
- *Sideways Stories from Wayside School* by Louis Sachar
- *The Substitute Teacher from the Black Lagoon* by Mike Thaler
- *Sylvester and the Magic Pebble* by William Steig
- *The True Story of the Three Little Pigs* by Jon Scieszka

Obviously, I'm not suggesting that you put all of these books into your bag of tricks at one time (you couldn't lift it off the floor!). Rather, select two or three books that will be appropriate for the class you are going to teach on any given day and put them in your bag.

Can I use these books for anything other than a "read aloud"?

Some of these titles are great for initiating a wonderful extension activity. For example, after reading *The True Story of the Three Little Pigs*, I told the students that we were going to have a "court session." I chose a student to play the Big Bad Wolf, and the rest of the class asked him questions for "testimony" to determine if he should be found guilty or innocent. Instant civics lesson!

The Keeping Quilt is a wonderful kickoff for an art project. Children can design and draw their own family quilts.

In almost every case, you can ask the children to analyze a book using a story map.

What is a story map?

After reading a story to the class, write the following on the board:

Title: _____

Author: _____

Setting: _____

_____

Problem: _____

_____

Solution: _____

_____

Sequence of Events: _____

    1. _____

    2. _____

    3. _____

Happy or Sad Ending? _____

Have students fill in the blanks with you or make their own form and complete it at their seats.

What should I do if I finish all planned lessons early?

I can still remember one of my first days as a sub. The classroom teacher had left me a sketchy plan for the day and, to be charitable, weak teaching materials and handouts. I did my best to present the material as effectively as I could, but as I glanced at the clock toward the end of the day, I knew that I'd finish early. I slowed down. I asked many questions. I did everything possible to s-t-r-e-t-c-h the final lesson so that the day would end when my teaching did. No luck! I finished and still had forty-five minutes until the final bell. What to do?

As a rookie sub, I hadn't yet learned the importance of the bag of tricks. My only option was to "tap dance." After exhausting all of my educational games and teaching a few songs, I left the class at 3:00 completely exhausted! And to be honest, I did not do very much to advance the curriculum. If

How do I handle a request to leave school early?

Dear Barbara,

Today I had an awkward situation. I was subbing in a fourth grade in a suburban school where the parents are very involved. It seems as if they flow in and out of the rooms all day long! They tend to be overly involved, in my opinion.

Yesterday, we had a classroom birthday party for Ashley. Her mother came in with cupcakes for the children and stayed to help me with the party. After the party was over, she wanted to take Ashley home immediately. It was 2:00 and the students are normally dismissed at 2:45. I was uncomfortable saying no, but I know the school has an early dismissal policy. I knew that the office must clear all students who go home early.

The mother was visibly irritated when I told her this, but I stood my ground! I had her report to the office for official clearance before I released Ashley to her. Was I wrong?

Christine in Connecticut

Dear Christine,

The dismissal policy established by the school is there for a reason. Parents have unfriendly divorces that often involve custody disputes over the children. For this reason, you must never dismiss any student without clearance from the office.

You did the right thing. If you had dismissed Ashley early, on your own, you would have violated a school rule. Always play it safe and follow safety procedures.

If the mother was unhappy with you and said you were being unreasonable, that's her problem. You are obligated to follow school procedures. You stood your ground and acted with authority. Being cautious was the right thing to do!

this were to happen to me today, I'd open my bag of tricks and have plenty of ammunition.

If you need to supplement the plans for the day, a wonderful lesson for the primary grades is to read a story to the class and then discuss the main idea and characters. Then students can write about their favorite parts of the story and draw pictures of a favorite character or event from the story. Or, you can have the students make a story map with you.

Your poetry book can be an introduction to a poetry lesson. Students can write a class poem (each child writes one line), or they may write their own poems and illustrate them. Because of the popularity of rap music, poetry is now very cool! Students can illustrate their poems and share them with classmates. I recommend using a book like *Where the Sidewalk Ends* by Shel Silverstein. The poems are funny and short, and students love them. They are a wonderful springboard for discussion and an example for creative writing activities.

The drawing book will help during transition times or when children have finished work early and have nothing to do. You may copy a page for them to work on, or you may draw the picture on the board, step-by-step, and have students work along with you. I have found the following technique to be very effective:

1. I draw a picture (using the step-by-step approach given in the how-to-draw book) on the board.
2. The students follow along at their desks.
3. I leave the picture on the board, letting them try it on their own.
4. When they have finished, they can color their pictures and write short stories about the characters they drew.

You can let early finishers work on the drawing activity and allow others to join in when they have completed their work. Or, you may want to use this technique as a reward for the end of the day, if you need to fill time.

As a sub, it's very important to avoid giving the students too much free time. Too much free time leads to disruption.

Once disruption starts, it is not easy to contain and get students back on track!

What's in the bag of tricks for middle school classes?

I've found that a key strategy for filling time is to get students talking about something that interests them. Yet abstract discussions (e.g., What do you like best about school?) are difficult to sustain. It's a better idea to have some props, and that's where your bag of tricks comes into play.

With time, you can build a file of interesting pictures for discussion. Try to find pictures that are photographically intriguing and at the same time tell a story. Ask the students what they think is happening. Then ask them to take one minute to try to memorize every detail in the picture. Remove the picture from sight and ask them to describe the picture in writing. If you'd like, you can have a contest to see who can remember the greatest number of specific details. Revisit the picture and examine what details were missed by everyone. Then discuss why they think that happened.

A book of short stories can also be a helpful tool and should be added to your bag of tricks. I've found that even though they wouldn't admit it publicly, most middle school students love to listen to stories, if the story is appropriate for their grade level. Try *Chicken Soup for the Teenage Soul* or *Reader's Digest* stories as starters. If you're adventurous, excerpts from Edgar Allan Poe or even Steven King might be appropriate. Over time, you'll find two or three books or stories that you know work well, and you can use them over and over. Just remember, the stories must be read theatrically if you expect to engage the students. Here is an opportunity to use your hidden acting talents!

What personal items should I place in my bag of tricks?

If it's properly stocked, your bag of tricks serves as your closet, your office, and your administrative assistant. It can provide you with food when you're hungry (pack sealed crackers in case there's no time for lunch), clothes for when you get wet or dirty (a spare shirt or blouse might be appropriate), entertainment when you have free time (a magazine or book), Band-Aids for foot blisters, deodorant for PE days, and any other personal emergency supplies.

I also suggest that you leave a pair of sneakers in your car. You may come to school and find out that you have been assigned PE for the day, or you may escort a group on a field trip. If you're wearing a pair of shoes that are terribly uncomfortable, you'll suffer for the entire day. It's easier to run out to your car to change into your comfortable extra pair of shoes.

Summary

Your bag of tricks is an emergency tool kit for subs. If you are assigned to a well-run classroom, you may never need it. However, on those days when you are left with no lesson plans or the plans are inadequate, you'll need to rely on your creativity and the trusty items in your bag of tricks. Be sure you follow these guidelines:

- Pack materials for all grade levels. You may think you're working in a first-grade class when you arrive, only to find out that you'll actually be subbing in a fifth-grade class.
- Be sure to pack a variety of school supplies and "specialty" items (e.g., a whistle, how-to-draw book, stickers).
- Have a few of your favorite books that will be appropriate for various grade levels as well as short stories for secondary school.
- Don't forget about your own comfort! Have some crackers just in case you are unable to buy lunch. Pack your personal comfort supplies as required.

When you arrive at school with a properly packed bag of tricks, you know that you've got "backup," just in case the day doesn't go as planned.

Classroom Management

Leslie Stone got to the classroom early. As a sub, she knew the importance of preparation before the class arrived. She needed time to study the schedule for the day and time to write her name on the board. She also knew it would be a good idea to greet the children individually as they entered the classroom.

Among the first children to enter was Daniel, a brown-haired fourth grader with a devilish grin. His eyes widened when he saw Leslie.

"Yeah! When we have a sub, we go crazy!" said Daniel.

Leslie smiled, well aware that "acting out" had become a common classroom reaction on sub days. She knew it was unrealistic to expect that she could change classroom culture in one day, but she would not allow disruptive behavior to ruin the day for the students or for herself.

When everyone arrived, Leslie introduced herself to the class, making sure she projected an aura of confidence.

"Good morning," she said confidently, making eye contact with as many children as possible. "My name is Ms. Stone, and I want you to know that I'm really happy to be your teacher today."

Leslie paused for just a beat to let the class hear the sound of silence.

"I've been a teacher—a real teacher—for many years," she said with a smile. "You look like you're an excellent class. I think we're going to have a wonderful day."

"I know you're going to work hard," she said. "I've brought some interesting activities and some really cool games and puzzles for you when your work has been completed."

The children began to buzz upon hearing about games and puzzles. Daniel pumped his fist and whispered, "Yes! Games."

Leslie looked directly at Daniel. "But the games and puzzles," she said with a friendly, but firm voice, "are a *reward* for hard work, and I'm sure, Daniel, you'll work hard to earn them."

Children make a very rapid collective assessment of you the moment they see you in a classroom. That's why I think it's so important to set a positive, authoritative tone at the start of the day. Most children feel relieved when a confident sub takes charge. It's scary to be in a room with no control.

Within the first few minutes, it's likely that one or two students will try to challenge your authority. They're testing for weakness, unconsciously trying to establish dominance. You have to win the first skirmish by being kind but firm. Issue your directions in a way that leaves no room for debate or argument.

A petite girl raises her hand, "Mrs. Camileri [the regular classroom teacher] always lets us switch seats so that we can work together."

Your reaction must be calm but firm. In a no-nonsense voice, you respond, "No, you may *not* switch seats for group work. Your teacher may let you work with your friends and that's great. But on sub days, we do things a little differently. Thank you for understanding."

All the begging in the world will not change your mind. The class sees that you are serious, and they are relieved. Someone is in control.

Should I try to make the class like me?

All of us want to be liked, and substitute teachers are no exception. But it's a mistake to try too hard to be liked by your students. There are times when your students *won't* like you, and that's okay!

Students are happiest when they feel safe and protected. It's your job to establish a safe and secure classroom environment, even if it means that your students feel that you're being authoritarian. "That's not fair" is a common exclamation when you work to avoid chaos (more about this later in the chapter). But a few frowns are a small price to pay in order to maintain control.

Remember, when chaos reigns in the classroom, everyone is miserable. The quiet, well-behaved children are uneasy, even frightened. And the boisterous few who are trying to disrupt the flow of the classroom aren't really happy. Someone needs to be the "heavy," and that someone is *you*! Even if the students don't like you for that instant, they will all feel better in a classroom that is calm and orderly.

Should I raise my voice or even yell if it's appropriate?

It's very important to understand that classroom management is *not* about yelling. In a firm, confident voice, you say, "No, that is *not* acceptable." Your tone and body language—your most important communication tools—telegraph the absolute expectation that your comments will be heeded. If the students try to ignore you, repeat yourself, calmly.

I recommend that as the volume of student voices goes up, your voice level should go *down*. A quiet, but strong voice in the midst of chaos can have a profound effect on those who hear it. It is *never* acceptable for students to ignore your words.

When order is restored (without yelling), you will be liked and respected for your strength and fairness. This is a wonderful feeling, and it is what makes you an effective substitute teacher.

How do I respond to "That's not fair"?

You will hear these words often, and as a sub, you must be careful not to fall into the trap of trying to be perfectly fair at all times to all students. Children may use these words to manipulate you, so be careful not to fall into the trap of defending yourself. You won't win!

Children sometimes feel that you are not being fair when they feel slighted or hurt. They want to turn a perceived injustice into revenge. And you are the tool!

I always tried to explain to the class that we all try to be fair, but they must understand that *life's not fair*. A good teacher tries to give each student what is best for that student, and what may be fair for one is not always the best for the next person. Sometimes we must do what is best for the whole group, and that may not feel fair to one or two individuals.

If the discussion about fairness continues, tell the students involved that you will discuss it and resolve the situation later, but now it is time to get back to work. Then you may take the children aside and resolve the problem privately.

A worthwhile discussion of fairness can be found in the book *Positive Discipline*.[1] The authors provide pragmatic solutions for handling situations in which students try to push your "fairness button."

How should I manage rewards and consequences?

In the classroom, a carrot is almost always better than a stick. Rewards provide positive reinforcement for good performance

---

1. Nelsen, J., et al. *Positive Discipline*. Three Rivers Press, 2001.

and good behavior. But rewards have to be balanced with consequences if performance or behavior is less than satisfactory. Use them both, and your ability to manage the classroom will be greatly enhanced.

The system that most good teachers establish encompasses both tiered rewards for good performance and behavior and a warning system with consequences for performance or behavior that doesn't meet school standards. Hopefully, there is a reward system in use in the classroom. Ask your special helper to explain it to you. (See the Helpers chapter.)

Many classrooms use multilevel warnings (e.g., green light, yellow light, red light) with consequences (e.g., write student's name in a special book, make a check next to name, miss recess, call the parent). If this approach is not effective for your needs that day, you will need a backup system.

There are many rewards systems that are effective. Here are a few that have worked for me. Try some of these and see which work best for you.

- **Recess as a reward.** On the board, write the word R-E-C-E-S-S in big letters. Tell the class that you will give them a recess period at the end of the day. However, if you need to remind them to be quiet, instead of telling them, you'll simply erase one letter of the word *recess* from the board. If the whole word is erased, recess is gone. However, even if just one letter is left, they are *safe*!
- **List of names.** Tell the class that their teacher has asked you to leave the names of any students who misbehave. However, say that you prefer to give the teacher a list of excellent students. You can write these names on the board or keep a list on paper. Just make sure all can see the list. Those on the list will be given a reward at the end of the day, and the names will be included in your teacher note.
- **Contest.** If the classroom is arranged in pods, rows, or sections, give each section a number. Each time a section is behaving well, put the number of the section on the board. Each time you want to compliment them, put a check next to that number. The section with the most checks will be

rewarded (e.g., stickers, treats, extra time for a free choice activity).

When children are arranged in groups and the whole group wants a reward, they will self-police. If one student is noisy, he can ruin the chance of a reward for the whole group. Usually one or more members of the group will act as your surrogate to quiet the noisy child. This can work for whole-class rewards as well.

Because you are not the classroom teacher, your survival tools are limited. I've found that if you use rewards effectively, they can make a real difference. So try some of the suggestions, and be on the lookout for others in the classrooms you visit.

But remember, always be consistent. If you start the day using a reward system, continue to use it throughout the entire day. Be sure that if you threaten consequences, you must be able to follow through.

There is much more that can be said about reward systems. In fact, entire books have been written on the subject. If you have additional interest, I recommend *Assertive Discipline* by Lee Canter and *The First Days of School* by Harry and Rosemary Wong.

Where should I sit/stand?

One of the best things you can do to maintain order is to circulate while students are working independently. Show an interest in their work, commenting on what you see. Compliment handwriting and content. A good sub *rarely* sits at the teacher's desk.

When giving a directed lesson, you should keep moving. Walk from side to side. Walk around and into the area occupied by the students' desks. If you see someone daydreaming, get into his or her space.

How do I know if my pacing is right?

You should begin the day with a personal introduction. (See the Introducing Yourself chapter.) As soon as the introduction

What happens if I learn something personal about a student's private life?

Dear Barbara,

I really enjoy teaching English at Orchard Middle School. Whenever the regular teacher is out, I'm called in to sub. I know most of the students, and they seem to like me.

All students in English class are asked to keep personal journals. Last week, Anna, a quiet young lady in the class, asked me to read her journal entry. I told her that I felt uncomfortable reading something private, but she insisted. At that point, I suspected she truly wanted me to see her entry.

As I read, I became alarmed at what I saw. She wrote about how she enjoyed cutting herself, and she described in great detail her nightly ritual of making small cuts on various places on her body.

I took her aside and expressed my concern. I was sure that she asked me to see her writing to open up a dialogue. We spoke briefly, and when she left, I knew I must do something to help her.

After careful consideration, I told the principal and the school guidance counselor. I also called the regular teacher that evening. I wanted them to know that this young lady needed help.

Was I wrong to betray a confidence?

Wendy in California

Dear Wendy,

The fact that your student, Anna, wanted to show you her writing is a tribute to you. She felt that you genuinely cared about her.

Cutting is a type of self-injury that is most common among adolescent girls, but some boys are involved in this behavior as well. Psychologists believe it is often a cry for help and provides a coping mechanism for dealing with strong emotions or depression. Unfortunately, cutting has become a new form of "cool" in some circles. Once started, cutting can become a compulsion.

You did the right thing by informing caring professionals in the school. The parents should also be notified. They should seek psychiatric help for their daughter.

Your actions in this situation were entirely appropriate and may very well have saved Anna from even more serious problems later.

is complete, begin the lesson immediately. You need to get the day started so that the students can see that you are there to teach and accomplish the goals of the classroom teacher.

Once your academic day has begun, pacing is important. If you move too slowly, children get bored. If you move too quickly, you'll lose some students. Even worse, you may finish with too much time to spare and then have time to fill—not a good thing!

Always pay attention to your students' faces and their body language. Try to sense where they are. If they seem very interested in the topic at hand, stretch out the discussion. Continue an activity or discussion when interest is high. Conversely, if they are wiggling in their chairs and looking bored, you need to adjust your pace accordingly.

What are the specific grade-level challenges?

Each age group presents its own challenges. An experienced sub is ready for all of them. After a few weeks of subbing, you will see patterns begin to emerge, and you will prepare yourself accordingly.

- **Primary grades.** Little ones are *needy*. Some will cry when they learn that their regular teacher is absent. You must be kind and nurturing in this environment. Reassure them that you are going to be their teacher for the day and that you promise Miss X will be back just as soon as she is feeling better. Compliment the class and tell them that Miss X must be a wonderful teacher to have such a great class. This calms them down and shows them that you are on their side. You are not the enemy!
- **Intermediate grades.** This age group is used to having subs and may see today as an opportunity to have a day off! You can assure them that they will have a great day, but everyone must get the work done that Mr. Y has left for them. I always promise that we'll do something special, but only *after* all work is completed. Be sure to have a story to read to them, an art project, or a quiet, organized game. (See the Bag of Tricks chapter.)

- **Middle school.** Dealing with older students is a special challenge and requires different techniques. As I noted earlier in this chapter, your first few minutes in the classroom are very important. Let the students know about your background and experience. Try to personalize your introduction by telling them something interesting about yourself, your family, or your career. You want them to see you as a person, not as an object. If possible, take the time to learn something about the content area that you will be teaching, if you have advance notice of the position for the day. Your knowledge of the subject matter gives you added credibility.

  As the day progresses, try to learn the names of as many students as possible (this applies to *all* grade levels). When you begin to address the students by name, it's likely that they will respond more readily to your requests and instructions.

  When confronted with disruptive behavior, avoid direct confrontation but use body language and a clear, firm tone to establish control. It's a good idea to use proximity to assist students with their tasks and to maintain order. Circulate throughout the classroom and be willing to help individuals.

  Most schools use referrals. These are slips of paper used to write up an individual. The student is then given a detention, or a day in a special room where he or she will be monitored. Find out if your school has this system, and plan on using it as a last resort. But don't threaten to use it if you do not plan on following through.

  A student with nothing to do will find something to keep himself busy, and that something may be disruptive to the classroom. For that reason, be sure to have some extra work for those who are off task. If one or two students are particularly disruptive, hand them a worksheet and tell them they must complete it before returning to the group. Make it a fairly simple exercise so that they will be able to complete it in five or ten minutes. If possible, offer a small reward for successful completion of the work.

Finally, recognize that the peer group is by far the most important thing in the life of a teenager. Do not feel hurt if you seem invisible to these students. It's not that they are rude or uncaring. They are consumed by their image, their friends, and their stature in the group. Learning about exponents is not the top priority when hormones are raging!

How do I handle students who represent a special challenge?

If a student is particularly challenging, a good strategy encompasses isolation and communication. First, isolate the student from others in the classroom. This may require taking the student to the back of the room or into the doorway so that you can keep an eye on the rest of the class. Once isolated, the disruptive student receives no feedback from others and often will calm down. Also, the student must face you—one-on-one.

Next, initiate communication by making direct eye contact. Ask whether there is a special problem. While looking directly into her eyes, indicate that you are unhappy and disappointed with the behavior. Tell her you do not want to embarrass her in front of classmates and suggest that a change in behavior begin "right now." Ask whether she understands what you've said.

These quiet, private talks can work wonders. When you take away the audience, and it's just the two of you, the student loses her incentive for misbehavior! Why show off if no one is watching?

When you return the student to the classroom setting, remove her from her current seat and place her in an area where she will not distract classmates. A referral may be needed if a challenging student continues to be uncooperative.

What is the best way to praise students at different grade levels?

Praise is a wonderful tool in the lower grades. Younger children thrive on it. I have found it to be the best reward possible.

Praise for the whole group is very powerful, and praise for small groups and individuals is equally effective.

Be aware that middle school students have an image to maintain. Sadly, being a nerd or the teacher's pet can be very embarrassing for the sixth grader who wants to maintain his or her cool image. In some communities, students will be ostracized if they are considered "too smart." So when you praise an older student, be subtle. Wait for a private time. If the student looks uncomfortable with your praise, sometimes a smile of recognition is just as effective.

Summary

Classroom management is profoundly important. A well-managed classroom allows you to teach and ensures that your students will have a good day. Be sure you follow these guidelines:

- Your initial introduction to the class is your opportunity to display your strength and competence. Use it to your best advantage.
- You may not always feel as if the students like you, and that is okay. Your job is to maintain order so that you will be able to teach.
- Use proximity to students to keep them on task.
- Be aware of your pacing by watching for student cues.
- Remember to use rewards and consequences consistently and fairly. A variety of reward systems are available for your use. When you have to threaten with consequences, be sure you follow through.
- If necessary, you may need to send in a referral on a very challenging student. Find out the procedure and use it as a last resort.

If you apply these guidelines effectively, you'll find yourself getting better at classroom management each time you sub!

Difficult Day

The minute Ed Bernard walked through the doorway, his wife, Jennifer, sensed something was wrong.

"How was your day, honey?" she asked.

Ed sighed, threw his knapsack gently on the kitchen table, and kissed their three-month-old daughter on the top of the head. "My day? It was just awful!"

Jennifer winced. "You want to talk about it?"

Ed took a kitchen chair and straddled it backward, resting his chin on the back of the chair. "I subbed in a fifth-grade class in a portable, no room for the backpacks, no place to isolate students who misbehaved. The principal was out sick. There were five students who decided to see how hard they could push me."

"Oh," said Jennifer softly. "There must have been a few good moments, no?"

Ed shrugged. "There were a few moments of peace and order. Then the noise would grow to an unacceptable level. All my old tricks failed me! Chaos reigned. By the end of the day, I just gave up. I kept looking at my watch, waiting for dismissal. I don't know how much longer I can do this."

It's obvious that substitute teacher Ed Bernard was discouraged after a difficult, exhausting day. He got off to a bad start because he had to work from plans that were very sketchy. Based on his comments, it's likely that he spent more time babysitting than teaching.

Here's the first period plan for social studies that Ed found on the classroom teacher's desk: *Have them work in groups on their projects. They know what to do.* For a sub, a plan like this can be a disaster. In Ed's case, most of the students told him that they were done with their projects. The few that were working had trouble concentrating because the others were fooling around.

When the classroom teacher is there to monitor group projects, a vague lesson plan is probably sufficient. But when children work in groups with a sub, the learning environment can degrade very quickly unless specific guidance is provided (to both the sub via plans and to the students via the sub). In general, I recommend that you try to avoid group work when you're subbing. Unless the group is carefully and closely managed, it can quickly get out of control with students fooling around or getting involved in off-task behavior.

Is it always my fault when order breaks down?

No, it isn't always your fault, and although difficult days are stressful, you should try not to let them become too discouraging. In a school and a classroom, things happen that are out of your control. Here are some examples.

- The regular classroom teacher may be having trouble establishing control in the classroom. A chaotic culture already exists, and then you walk in the door. If the classroom teacher has not established good classroom routines and behavior standards, it is nearly impossible for you to change those standards in one day.

- The classroom teacher did not prepare for her absence—no lesson plans, no class list, hidden teaching materials, no seating chart. How can you be effective if you don't even know the names of the students?
- One or more students may be having outside issues that affect their in-school behaviors. Perhaps a child just had a horrendous argument with a parent. That child sees you as another authority figure and decides to act out against you. Of course, you have no way of knowing the reason for the behavior.

Sometimes, you just have to accept that even with your best effort, the day is going to be difficult. On such an occasion, try to focus on the students who are behaving. Reward them with your attention, give them your praise, and have them help you with classroom chores.

Is there any way to recover after a bad start?

Yes, and it's definitely worth a try! First, do a self-check. Are you following the guidelines I've suggested?

- Does your body language project self-assurance?
- Are you using a calm, but authoritative voice?
- Are you maintaining good eye contact with students?
- Are you projecting a caring demeanor and a good sense of humor?
- Are you acting with consistency and following through?

If your self-check is positive, focus on the class itself. Perhaps you have not lost the whole group. Is there one particular student who is causing the disruption? If so, isolate that child and have a firm talk with him. If you see no change, write a referral or send him to the office. These actions show other children that you are serious and will not tolerate poor behavior.

If the plans or material that you were given are too difficult or too unstructured, you can still save the day. Finish up quickly, or put that work aside, and try an activity from your bag of tricks. You're familiar with the materials in your bag and can present them with assurance. It will be a welcome change and may get the class back on track.

What should I do if I am asked to show a video that doesn't engage the students?

In order to avoid writing a detailed lesson plan, some classroom teachers may ask you to show a video to the class. They may even convince themselves that showing a video will make your life easy as well. But if the video is wrong for the age group, has been shown before, or is unacceptably dry and uninteresting, the class will lose interest. This situation occurs all too frequently and can result in classroom management problems.

I was asked to sub for a music teacher, and part of her "plan" asked me to show a video of the movie *Mary Poppins*, which worked fairly well for the younger children. But when I started the video for fourth and fifth graders, they moaned and groaned and started laughing. It was immediately apparent that *Mary Poppins* would have to go! I turned off the video, and thinking fast, I asked the students to make up a TV commercial—with music—for their favorite breakfast cereal. When they finished, each cereal commercial was presented to the class. A few students said they did not want to do that, so I handed them a word search with musical terms. All were busy, the students were engaged, and the class remained relatively calm and quiet.

What if I never restore order?

Usually, the classroom will settle down in time. Be cool under fire, moving from one proven subbing technique to another in an effort to find something that will work. If the classroom is chaotic, try to find the instigator, isolate her, and have a private conversation. If the child is incorrigible, write a refer-

How should I handle an uncooperative classroom aide?

Dear Barbara,

I often sub in a room where the teacher's aide has an attitude. She sits on her chair and does nothing. The student that she is assigned to help (a boy with ADHD) becomes disruptive because he is not getting the help he needs. I'm sure when the regular teacher is in school, the aide does her job, but when I'm in the room, she decides to take the day off.

I have asked her for help, but she gives me "a look," gets off the chair slowly, and walks to her student. It's gotten to the point where I feel uncomfortable asking her to help.

It is not in my nature to be confrontational, but it seems unfair to the child, the other students, and me! This teacher's aide is making my life miserable! How should I handle it?

Gail in Minnesota

Dear Gail,

I can understand how you must feel. People like the teacher's aide you are describing have a distinct way of intimidating others.

But remember, you are in charge of that classroom for the day. It is just as important to guide the teacher's aide as it is to guide your students. Classrooms run smoothly when the teacher controls the flow.

You need not be confrontational. With a take charge tone, you must tell her that her assistance is needed right now, and, if necessary, remind her frequently. If she gives you her "look," ignore it. Pretend you didn't see it. If you display an aura of confidence, you leave her no choice but to do her job.

It's important for you to feel comfortable in your subbing assignments. Establish your role with confidence each day. If an aide is with you, express your respect for her, thank her in advance, but be a clear leader in that classroom.

ral or call the office for help. My suggestions in the Classroom Management chapter will be of use as well.

If the day continues to be miserable, please remember that one difficult day is just that—one bad day. Tomorrow will be better. You may be assigned to your favorite third grade class. The children will be happy to see you, and they may ask you to read them the same story that you read to them the last time you were in for a visit. That special child who remembers your kindness from the last visit will make you a card with hearts and rainbows. You'll smile and forget about the previous difficult day.

Summary

Difficult days happen whether you're a doctor, lawyer, firefighter, or substitute teacher. They're part of the job, and you can't take them too seriously.

You will have bad days, and, most of the time, they will not be your fault. The culture of a classroom may not be ideal, one difficult student can be extremely disruptive, lesson plans may be below par, or name tags or seating charts may not be available. Your fault? I don't think so!

When things begin to unravel in the classroom, follow these simple guidelines:

- Do a self-check to ensure that you're doing the things that lead to classroom control.
- Focus on the classroom dynamic, trying to understand why things are going awry and what you might be able to do to correct the situation.
- Evaluate the subject matter. If it's too complex or simply "not right" for this moment in time, get through it and move on to something that might change the classroom atmosphere in a positive way.

When all strikes are against you, survival is your goal. Do the best that you can, but don't be too hard on yourself. Tomorrow will be better!

Ethics

The teacher lounge is a place to relax, and that's exactly what sixth-grade teacher Colin McKenzie was doing while his students were at gym. In addition to Colin, I sat chatting and drinking coffee with two other subs. Another teacher, Alisha Gold, walked in with an agitated look on her face.

Colin looked up and noticed her agitation. "Hey, Alisha, you look frazzled. What's up?"

Alisha frowned. "I can't stand the way Matthew Wooden behaves in my room," she said in a stage whisper. "He's so sneaky. Whenever there's an item missing, I check his desk and there it is. My goodness, he even takes pencils and lunch money from other kids."

Colin nodded knowingly. "Well, the apple doesn't fall far from the tree. Didn't you know that his dad is in prison for stock fraud?"

Alisha gasped. "I had no idea!"

Even though this conversation occurred in the privacy of the teacher's lounge, both Colin and Alisha made a number of ethical mistakes and showed very poor judgment.

First, the student who was exhibiting problem behavior was identified by name in front of another teacher. It is not ethical or appropriate to discuss a student's problems within the school community or with visitors or other parents.

Second, other personnel were within earshot and were now privy to the student's problems. They might unfairly prejudge other siblings of the child or spread rumors about the family. After all, teachers are human.

Third, a serious family issue (the father's plight) was divulged. The children and the family expect and deserve privacy.

All of us like to talk about our work, and teachers are no different. But it is not ethical to discuss the name of a child who goes to the Resource Room, sees the school psychologist, or has special needs. Children deserve respect and privacy, and so do their families.

Of course, there's more to ethics than a legitimate concern for privacy. In this chapter, I'll try to provide you with a quick primer on ethical behavior for subs.

What are "ethics," and how should they be applied?

Most states have a written Code of Ethics and Professionalism that outlines the ethical standards for teachers. As a sub, you should be aware of these standards and follow them in your dealings with children. Although every state takes a slightly different approach to this issue, a number of important ethical guidelines almost always appear.

- Protect children from conditions harmful to learning and keep them safe.
- Be aware of Occupational Safety and Health Administration and Food and Drug Administration (OSHA/FDA) precautions. Follow guidelines for blood borne pathogens. Do not touch or have students touch

bodily fluids. When there is an accident, let the nurse handle it. She is knowledgeable and prepared.
- When you are on recess duty, keep your eyes on the students at all times.
- If you sense at any time that a student might become violent, call the office immediately.
- Never leave the classroom unattended. If you must leave to go to the bathroom, ask the teacher next door to watch your class.
- Protect students from unnecessary embarrassment, harassment, and discrimination.

It is as important to keep children psychologically safe as it is to keep them physically safe. I was teaching a second-grade class when a little boy bent over and ripped the seat of his pants. No one noticed but me. I quickly stood behind him and had him come into the doorway, shielding his back from view. I knew that if the children saw his underwear, it would give them an opportunity to tease him mercilessly.

Once he was safely out of sight, I gave him a jacket to tie around his waist as he marched to the office. I then alerted the office to call a parent to send in a new pair of pants.

In our diverse culture, it is not unusual for discriminatory behavior to rear its ugly head. If you see one student harassing or discriminating against another because of race, religion, or sexual orientation, you must act immediately. When I have been witness to "ugly" talk like this, I take the rude child aside and talk privately about how hurtful his or her language is. I also say that I intend to tell his teacher about it and suggest a phone call to the parent. If the hurtful behavior continues, send the child to the office or write up a referral. Bullying and teasing must never be tolerated.

Here are some additional guidelines for ethical behavior:

- **Respect the privacy of students, their parents, and your colleagues.** When you enter a school, you are a professional. Just as a lawyer or psychiatrist will not divulge a confidence, a teacher should maintain the same standards for student confidentiality and privacy. *What happens in school stays in school!*

- **Maintain honesty with colleagues and children.** Brian Walton was a small man with a slight lisp, eyeglasses, and a meek demeanor. When he began subbing, Brian thought he'd invent a new image, a background that would impress and possibly even frighten the children so that they would behave well in his class. From the moment the students entered his room, Brian acted like a tough guy, telling the students he had a background in law enforcement. He bragged about his experience using all kinds of deadly weapons (completely inappropriate), trying to frighten the children into submission! His stories were so outrageous that the students knew he was lying. Children are perceptive and can spot a phony a mile away. Always be genuine.
- **Be punctual, be dependable, and dress professionally.** Try to arrive at least one half hour before the children, giving yourself enough time in the morning to read over the schedule and plans for the day. You'll create problems for yourself if you run into the classroom just as the students arrive. Punctuality pays.

  Dependability is a key attribute that leads to repeat subbing assignments. If you commit to an assignment in advance, be sure to be there on time and with a smile on your face. Don't cancel. People are depending upon you. If you're unreliable, you will not be called again.

  I have always found that dressing well commands respect. A man in a button-down shirt and tie looks like a *real* teacher, not a sub. Women should wear a skirt or dress pants, a blouse or sweater, and closed shoes. The more professional you look and act, the more respect you will get. As subs, we need all the help we can get, and dressing well is a painless way to get it. You don't need to spend a lot of money on your sub wardrobe. Discount clothing stores are loaded with nice apparel for teaching.

What happens if I have no time to prepare?

Dear Barbara,

I arrived a half an hour early for my subbing assignment (which is expected) as a math teacher. Normally, this routine gives me plenty of time to look over the day's plans.

When I checked in at the office, the principal asked me if I would mind taking bus duty. She explained that generally this job is not given to a sub, but many teachers were away for in-service training and they were shorthanded.

Being a flexible person, I said, "Of course, glad to help!" Bus duty was easy, and I was glad that I was able to be of assistance.

When I entered my fifth-grade class, the students were filing in. They approached me with permission slips and questions about the previous night's homework. I felt as if I couldn't catch my breath. Before I knew it, I heard the Pledge of Allegiance and morning messages on the PA system. Math instruction was next.

The math lesson was on perimeter and circumference. Of course these topics are not difficult, but this content area is one that I needed to review before teaching. Concepts like pi = 3.14, diameter, radius, and circumference were included in the lesson. Some students got it immediately, but many struggled.

Being mathematically impaired, I was totally flustered and forgot some important details of the content area. Any suggestions?

Samantha in Virginia

Dear Samantha,

In an ideal world, you would have reviewed the math terms and gone over the problems in advance. You might have been able to do a Web search on math curriculum for Grade 5 and found some extra worksheets for students who finished early as well as some for those that needed extra help.

Since you had bus duty that morning, time was not on your side. When a situation like this occurs, try to delay the math lesson by giving the students a ten-minute assignment of independent work, such as a review page, journal writing, or a problem of the day.

While they are busy, review the material for yourself. Find the Teacher's Guide and do the first few problems to gain experience and refresh your memory. When you feel ready, begin the lesson. It's always better to appear prepared. If you stumble during the first few minutes of the day, you lose respect instantly and it may be difficult to recover.

After doing the first few problems on the board, ask volunteers to come up and do the next few. Now you are in control, and students will see that you have some knowledge of the content.

Boy Scouts and substitute teachers share a motto: Be Prepared.

What are crisis codes?

Many schools have become proactive about *critical incidents*. These include events like school shootings, bomb threats, and explosive devices. If you attend a substitute teacher orientation, you will learn about this important issue. If not, it would be wise to ask in the school office. Find out if there is a written pamphlet on crisis codes. The codes are usually represented with colors, building up from Code White (a minor incident) to Code Red (a major incident demanding full lockdown).

Full lockdown means that there will be no movement in the building except for police or fire officials. There will be evacuation plans that may be announced on the school PA. Usually the students are aware of these rules, but as a professional, it is your duty to learn the crisis code procedures required in your school.

What are the legal issues of subbing?

Many teachers (myself included) sometimes have the uneasy feeling that fear of litigation has changed the school environment and teaching—and that the change is not necessarily for the better. However, it is the teacher's obligation to follow the dictates of the school district in order to avoid legal entanglements. Among many guidelines in this area are:

- **Never touch a student.** The climate in our society frowns on physical contact of any kind. In the lower grades this is difficult to enforce. Young children want to hug you and hold your hand. You must use good judgment here. In middle school the rule is clear. Play it safe, keep your distance, and follow the rule of no touching.
- **Never discuss your personal religious or political views or try to persuade students to follow them.** Although it is perfectly fine to discuss politics or religion if such topics are relevant to the subject matter being taught, it is unethical to proselytize in any way.
- **Never use language or act in any manner that could be interpreted as sexual harassment.** Be especially careful of inappropriate humor, improper references to a student's appearance, or any comment that could have a double meaning.
- **If you witness an accident, be sure to report it to the office.** The school nurse will prepare an accident report and will ask for your input.

If I suspect child abuse, should I report it?

School employees (including substitute teachers) are instructed to notify school administrators if they have any suspicion of neglect or abuse. Administrators and other professionals are trained to handle the situation properly. If you suspect neglect or abuse, the first person you should notify is your principal. You need not have irrefutable proof, but I do recommend that you document any conversation or other evidence that caused you to report possible abuse or neglect.

What is a drug-free workplace?

Most school districts and boards of education have a written policy about smoking, drugs, and alcohol. There will be no possession or distribution of controlled substances.

Employees who violate the drug-free workplace policy will be subject to disciplinary action. As a sub, it is very important that you adhere to these rules and regulations.

Should I participate when teachers gossip?

You walk into the teachers' lounge and a few teachers are gossiping about the messy divorce that the parents of a student are going through. You've subbed at this school many times, live in the community, and know everyone present as well as the student. Two members of the group motion for you to join them, anxious to get your input. They know that you socialize with the family.

You don't want to seem antisocial, and, besides, you like these teachers. But you feel uncomfortable indulging in gossip. How should you proceed?

Teachers are human, and more than a few like nothing better than to share the latest "dirt" about a colleague, an administrator, or a student. It's not something our profession is proud of, but it does happen.

As a sub, you will be exposed to this behavior. My advice is simple: Do not indulge in it!

But the gossiping group may press you for an opinion. Try the following response: "I've met student X's parents a few times, and I feel bad about their situation. They are good people. I feel really uncomfortable discussing it. I hope you understand." You've gently removed yourself from the conversation and maintained your dignity. You will be respected for it!

What is my role in the school and community?

It's a bright spring day and you're walking through the parking lot of the local grocery store, about a half mile from a school that you sub in regularly and only a quarter mile from your house. Deep in thought, you're approached by someone who calls your name. It's your longtime neighbor, Lin Jackson.

After a few pleasantries, Lin says, "You know, I'm really concerned about Ms. Monaco."

The neighbor is referring to her son's third-grade teacher at Peck School—the same school where you subbed that day.

Before you can respond, the neighbor goes into a two-minute diatribe about Ms. Monaco and ends with, "What do you think of her?"

Your response should sound something like this. "You sound really upset, Lin, and I sympathize. But it would be unethical for me to discuss any teacher at the school. I work there, too, you know."

As a sub, it's not at all unusual to live in the same community in which you work. Your friends and neighbors may be tempted to ask your opinion about other students, school personnel, or school politics. Be extremely cautious.

Summary

Every substitute teacher is expected to behave ethically and treat students, parents, and colleagues with respect. Today, ethics is a major point of emphasis in school systems nationwide. You'll never have ethical difficulties if you follow these guidelines:

- Protect children from conditions harmful to learning and keep them safe.
- Make yourself aware of school crisis codes and OSHA/FDA standards.
- Adhere to the drug-free workplace policy.
- Protect students from unnecessary embarrassment, harassment, and discrimination.
- Respect the privacy of students, their parents, and your colleagues.
- Be honest with colleagues and with the students.
- Be punctual, be dependable, and dress professionally.

- Avoid gossiping with professional colleagues and with outsiders who want your opinion about school-related subjects.
- Be aware of the legal ramifications of your actions at all times.

In every case, follow all school board ethics guidelines. They have been developed to protect you from the truly unpleasant consequences that can occur when ethics are breached.

First Time in a School

It was almost 8:05 in the morning, and substitute teacher Amy Proper should have been taking attendance in her sixth-grade classroom at J. M. Henderson School. Instead, she was wandering the maze of hallways looking for Room 426. She winced as the morning bell rang and looked desperately at her watch.

As she rounded the corner of yet another hallway, Amy almost tripped over the school custodian who was on his knees, fixing a broken hallway tile.

"Thank goodness," Amy exclaimed. "Can you tell me where I can find Room 426?"

The custodian looked up slowly, "Who are you, a parent? Did you check in at the office? They're supposed to take you to the classroom."

Amy raised her hands to stop him. "Uh, no. I'm a sub, and I, uh, I'm lost."

"Fifth room on the right," said the custodian as he looked back down at the broken tile.

As she arrived at the room she didn't need to check the number. She heard the children inside, enjoying themselves in the absence of teacher supervision. It took her fifteen minutes to get them to quiet down.

Not a good start.

Your first day in any new environment can be confusing. That's why in the business world many companies provide orientation sessions and assign a coworker to guide any new person through the day. Unfortunately, in education, although you may attend a sub orientation, you'll rarely, if ever, have a mentor or coworker to help you. You arrive for your first day at a school, and you're expected to know your way around the building, to be familiar with local rules and regulations, and to magically adapt to the idiosyncrasies of faculty and staff—a tall order to be sure!

There are, however, some concrete things you can do to avoid problems that will arise because of your unfamiliarity with a new environment. In this chapter, I'll discuss some of the ways that you can make your first day easier.

Is there anything I can do before my first assignment at the school?

Most schools have websites that contain useful information about the school and its people. If you have time, be sure to visit the website. You can familiarize yourself with the school layout, get driving directions if you need them, learn the names of administrators and staff, and get a general feel for the school itself. None of this will make you an expert, but it will help you to acclimate yourself more quickly when you do arrive.

What should I do when I walk through the front door?

Try to arrive early and introduce yourself to the contact person in the office. A cheerful demeanor is very important. You're an outsider; it's up to you to establish rapport.

The people in the front office can be your best allies or your worst nightmare. You may need them for assistance throughout the day, so it's important to get them on your side. To do this, make an effort to learn each of their names, and then use their names throughout the day. Smile a lot, defer to their suggestions whenever possible, be apologetic if you ask for assistance, and never, ever project a master-servant attitude. If you plan to sub at a number of different schools, write down the names of office staff at each school and review the list before your day begins.

What should I say when I walk into the office?

You walk into a busy administration office at the beginning of the day. Teachers are walking in and out, parents with special requests are standing at the counter, the assistant principal is visible in his or her glass enclosed office, and the staffers are looking harried and not completely awake.

"Hi," you say with a smile, trying to make eye contact with the closest office staff person. "I'm Ms. X and I'll be subbing for Mr. Z today."

The staffer looks up and frowns. "Just a sec, and I'll be right with you."

You notice that the nameplate on her desk identifies her as Melinda Harold, and you repeat her name silently to yourself.

"You're a sub?" says Melinda with little emotion.

Again you smile. "Yes. I'll be subbing for Mr. Z. It's my first time in the school, so . . . if you have a map of the rooms?"

"I have one here someplace," responds Melinda. "Here it is."

"You know," you say, "I had some education classes at State U with a Jennifer Harold. She's not a relation, is she?"

Melinda brightens. "Oh my, yes, she's my niece. She's graduating this year. We're all very proud of her."

"Tell her that I said hi."

"I will, for sure. Have a good day, and if you need anything at all, just see me. Here, let me show you the fastest way to get to Room 118."

Melinda is smiling broadly now. You've engaged her, and you have an ally in the office.

Before you leave, you decide to take advantage of Melinda's generous offer of help.

"Ms. Harold," you begin.

"Oh, just call me Melinda. Everyone else does."

"Melinda, can you tell me about the sign-in and sign-out procedure?"

Sign-in and sign-out procedures vary from school to school. Most schools have very strict rules for visitors, so be sure to follow the procedure exactly. Many schools ask you to sign in on a computer and to wear a badge for the day.

Once you arrive at your classroom, your special student helper can help you navigate through early morning activities and can also help you find the rooms for specials, the cafeteria, and the restrooms. (See the Helpers chapter.) If the school has a particularly complex layout, try to notice landmarks that will help you retrace your steps.

Should I introduce myself to other teachers?

It is extremely important to introduce yourself to the teacher in the room next door. Chances are that classroom will be the same grade level, and the teacher will have knowledge of the curriculum and routines. You'll welcome that person's help. The teacher in the room next door might also have been given specific information for you by the teacher for whom you are subbing.

If you return to the same school shortly after, be sure to make contact with the classroom teacher for whom you subbed. Teachers love to hear about and talk about their students, so have a few comments ready and don't be afraid to compliment the class. It's likely that part of the conversation will follow this pattern:

How do I handle a classroom culture of "no rewards, but plenty of consequences"?

Dear Barbara,

What do you do when you are subbing in a room where the behavior management system consists of only consequences, with no rewards?

Each time I sub for Ms. Y's first grade, she makes a point of reminding me about the "traffic light" and clips with children's names for naughty behavior. It's a fine system, but I feel there's something missing. There's no way to reward good behavior. As a result, the students are unruly and it's very difficult to get them to settle down. I feel that I should use the system that's in place, but I need some tools for positive reinforcement. Any ideas?

Jim in New Jersey

Dear Jim,

Establishing consequences for negative behavior is certainly a necessary part of any behavior management system. But a sub needs to have a system for positive reinforcement also.

When you consistently point out negative actions, the children become accustomed to that type of feedback. There are children who thrive on attention, be it negative or positive. For these children, even negative feedback is better than no feedback. I suggest that you have a few reward systems in place. Here are some ideas:

1. For the younger children, give out stickers when you see exemplary behavior. Make a big deal out of presenting the stickers, and tell them you have more to give out throughout the day. A word of caution: be selective or the stickers will lose their impact.
2. Tell the class that you are keeping a detailed list of students who are cooperative. Each time you see a student following directions, helping a friend, and so on, put a check next to his or her name. The boy and girl with the most checks will get to pick out a prize from your bag of tricks at the end of the day. A few visits to a dollar store and you will have pencils, erasers, notepads, and other goodies that kids love!
3. Give a "whole class" reward. If the whole class gets ten points on the board for everyone being on task, they will get an extra five minutes of recess or free time.

4. Have a handful of tickets. Give them out when you see someone "being good." The tickets can be traded in for a prize at the end of the day.
5. A variation on the ticket plan—whoever has the most tickets at the end of the day gets a prize.

By the way, a reward system may be nice for the students, but the real "reward" is for you—a manageable class!

Classroom teacher: How did Seth behave for you? He usually gives subs a hard time. He drives me crazy some days!

You: Seth wasn't too bad on Monday, but I can see what you mean. He tried to challenge me a few times. I can imagine what you must go through.

A conversation like this shows that you are truly interested in the students. You will appear to be a caring individual who empathizes with the teacher's situation. That teacher will probably request you the next time he or she is absent.

I have found that there are teachers in each school who try to make conversation with the subs and others who don't bother because you are not part of their daily life. It's not your job to meet every individual in the building, but try to introduce yourself when appropriate. You want to appear friendly and caring.

Summary

Walking into a school for the first time as a sub is never easy, but it is manageable. By following these simple guidelines, you can always get off to a good start:

• Do some research to learn about the school before your first visit. Most schools have websites, and it's always worth a few minutes of your time to check them out.

- Try to arrive early. There may be some confusion surrounding your first visit to a new school. You don't want to be late for class.
- Be sure to cultivate a good relationship with front office staff. They can help you get over the hurdles of being a "newbie."
- Introduce yourself to the teacher in the room next door. You may need some special information about routines and curriculum.

Each school has its own culture. Prepare in advance, be an astute observer, and be friendly to faculty and staff, and the next time your visit will be easy!

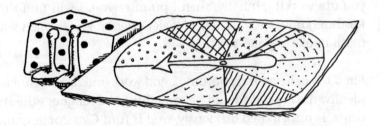

Games

Regina Rich had subbed in this classroom before, and the children obviously remembered her. As she walked toward the teacher's desk, a quiet murmur rose among the students.

Regina placed her bag on the desktop and turned to face the class. She looked out over a sea of expectant faces, wrote her name and the date on the board, and smiled. "I'm Ms. Rich. I hope you remember me. I certainly remember all of you."

She acknowledged a girl whose hand had been raised from the moment she saw Regina at the classroom door. "Yes, Miranda, right?" (Regina has a remarkably good memory for names.)

The girl smiled broadly. "You remembered me! Cool."

"May I help you, Miranda?" asked Regina.

"Oh, please, please, please can we play Higher/Lower, Ms. Rich? The last time you were here, I didn't get a chance to play. I want a turn today."

"Perhaps we'll have time for that before lunch," said Regina gravely. She paused for a moment, looking at each child. "But I need all of you to *earn* that privilege. If we can get through the work that Mr. Marino has assigned for you and I see that you are working quietly, then I promise you, I will find time for that game before lunch. Now let's begin. Please open your math books to page 167."

I'm a big believer in rewarding good work and good behavior. Ideally, the reward should be something that engages the students, is anticipated anxiously, and is fun! Classroom games are often a wonderful reward.

When substitute teacher Regina Rich taught her fourth-grade class a game called Higher/Lower, she used it as a reward. The children loved it, and as soon as they saw her they were reminded of the nice time they had. The game was her hook!

Is it appropriate to play games?

Classroom teachers don't want subs to spend the day solving puzzles, handing out word finds, and playing games. After all, serious educational work needs to be accomplished. In the modern school environment with the emphasis on testing and accountability, there is enormous pressure to cover the curriculum, often to the exclusion of extracurricular activities.

However, there will be days when you are given no plans, or other days when you complete the plans with time to spare. It is at these times that games can serve as both a filler and as an incentive for the students to complete their work in a timely and cooperative manner. When you play a game, you are in control, and if you choose the right games, learning will occur. So, it is appropriate to play games, but be sure you choose your games wisely.

How can games be educational?

Any game that is played in the classroom should have three attributes:

1. It must be fun.
2. It must be age appropriate.
3. It must have some educational merit.

The games that I recommend in this chapter have all three attributes. They are fun; if chosen properly, they can be targeted to a specific age group; and they all require solid thinking skills.

It's important to note that games can also be used to complement the curriculum. Games can be used to review spelling words and vocabulary. They can be used to review concepts that prepare students for tests. Math games can be used to review facts and hone skills.

Whenever possible, try to adapt classic classroom games to fit into your curriculum. Later in the chapter, I'll suggest some things that will help you accomplish this.

When should I play games?

Games can become an important element of your classroom management approach. Therefore, use them to your advantage. It's best to introduce a game early in the day, during a quiet time when you know it will be well received. Play it once or twice and then stop. Promise the students that you'll repeat the game later in the day, but only if they exhibit good work habits and behavior.

What types of classroom games are available?

There are many websites with school appropriate games for all age groups. (See the Web Resources chapter.) Here is a list of classroom games that are winners! They require some thinking skills, and they reinforce learning.

- **Spelling Bee.** Aside from the classic version, you can modify the traditional Spelling Bee for math problems or to review facts for a test. Ask the class how they line up for a Spelling Bee (methods vary). If they say they never have Spelling Bees, you can line them up by teams, randomly, or by rows, and have students sit down when they miss a word. The team left with the last person standing is the winner.
- **Sparkle.** A variation on the Spelling Bee, Sparkle can be a great way to drill spelling or vocabulary words in a challenging way. The class forms a circle and is given a word. The first student says the first letter, the next says the second letter, and so on. When a student provides the wrong letter, he or she sits down. When the word is completed, the next person says "Sparkle" and the very next person must sit down. Play continues until only one student is left standing . . . the winner!
- **Hangman.** This classic is always well received. Think of a vocabulary word or a term from geography, science, or any other subject. Draw dashes on the board corresponding to the number of letters in the word. Now draw a "gallows."

  Students then guess a letter that might be in the word. If the letter appears in the word, it is placed in its proper position over a dash, but if the guess is wrong, draw a head, stick figure body, arms, and legs (one at a time for each bad guess) under the gallows. The student who figures out the word is the next person to come to the

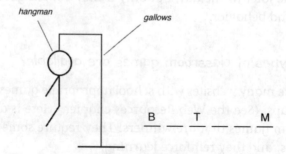

hangman   gallows

board and think of the next word. However, if the body is complete, with all body parts hanging from the gallows, then the teacher has won and will make up the next word. Try to judge your group. It may be best if you continue to be the person at the board making up the words. If the group seems mature, you can allow the students to take turns with this task.

- **Scrambled Letters.** Write a word on the board with the letters out of order. Have students unscramble them to find the correct word. The first student who comes up with the correct word wins. Variations: Use names of the students, teachers in the school, or famous sports figures, or use a science or social studies term.

- **How Many Words?** Write a word on the board and see how many smaller words you can make from the letters in the larger word. Have children write the smaller words on their own pieces of paper and then read them to the class. Whoever has the most words is the winner. Set a time limit of five minutes.

- **Charades.** This classic party game can be modified for classroom use by choosing a student to go to the front of the room and act out a well-known song, movie, or book title. To maintain decorum, it's a good idea to have students raise their hands to offer a guess instead of shouting out the answers. Whoever guesses correctly has the next turn.

  A variation of Charades for the primary grades is to act out spelling words or vocabulary words from the content area. When I play this game with my younger students, I whisper or write down the suggested word to the "actor." That person goes to the front of the room and begins to act out the spelling word. If a student in the class thinks he or she knows what the word is, that student raises a hand and guesses. If he or she is correct, that student takes a turn acting out another word.

- **Around the World.** Choose a leader from among your students. The leader stands beside the first child in the first row. Using a set of flash cards (e.g., math facts), stand in front of both children, holding up one flash card. The child that gives you the correct answer first wins that round. He or she then moves to the next child, and the same process is repeated with a new flash card. If the child sitting beats the child standing, the two students change places with child #1 sitting in the seat of child #2. If one student can go "around the world" (meaning that student beats every other student in the class), he or she is the winner.

- **Twenty Questions.** When I played this game with my students, I always went first. I would choose a scorekeeper to write the tally marks on the board to be sure we did not exceed twenty questions. To begin play, think of an animal, vegetable, or mineral (you might need to explain the differences). Then have children pose questions to you requiring a yes or no answer. You may only answer with a yes or no.

  Based on the answers to the questions, students may guess what you're thinking. The student who guesses correctly wins and becomes the next person to challenge the class.

  To make this game more educational, try to choose a word or term that relates to the current curriculum. For example, if the students are studying astronomy or space, you might choose one of the planets or constellations as your challenge.

- **Higher/Lower.** One student stands at the board, facing the class. The teacher writes a number on the board above the student's head so that it can't be seen by the student. The student at the board guesses a number. Classmates say "higher" or "lower," indicating which direction to go to find the number written on the board. Once the child has guessed correctly, he or she chooses the next student to go to the board. The number range varies by age group. In Kindergarten, Grade 1, and Grade 2, make your numbers 0–100. With Grades 4 and up, you can use numbers with a range of thousands to one million. The game is best for students in Kindergarten through fourth grade.

- **The Unique Game.** Ask the children what *unique* means.
  You will get many interesting answers. Then put a positive
  spin on the word. Tell them that it is very special to be a
  unique person.

  Now explain the rules of the game. Tell the students
  that they must be truthful. If not, they will ruin the
  game. For this reason, the Unique Game is generally not
  appropriate for Kindergarten or first-grade students.

  The entire class stands next to their desks. You suggest
  characteristics that would describe one or more students.
  If the characteristic applies to a student, he or she must
  sit down. The characteristics (which may be posed as
  questions) are fun personal things that you would have no
  way of knowing. A few suggestions:
  1. Did you have cereal for breakfast? If you did, please sit
     down.
  2. Did you have toast for breakfast? If you did, please sit
     down.
  3. Are you the oldest child in your family? If yes, please
     sit down.
  4. If you are having hot lunch today, please sit down.
  5. If you brought a sandwich from home, please sit down.
  6. Did you go to an overnight camp this summer? If you
     did, please sit down.
  7. If you went to Disneyland or Disney World this year,
     please sit down.
  8. Do you have a younger brother in this school? If yes,
     please sit down.
  9. Do you have a younger sister in this school? If you do,
     please sit down.
  10. Is your birthday is August? If yes, please sit down.
     (Name other months to eliminate people).

     When only one child is left standing, the game is over.
  That person wins because he or she is the most unique.
- **Seven Up.** This game is a favorite in elementary school.
  Choose seven children to stand in front of the room.
  Choose a light monitor to turn the lights on and off for
  you. Say, "Lights out, heads down." All other students

put their heads down and close their eyes. The seven now tiptoe around the room and each taps one child's head. When all seven have finished this task, they return to the front of the room.

Turn on the lights. Announce, "Heads up."

Each child whose head was tapped stands up. One at a time, they announce who they think tapped their heads. If they guess correctly, they replace that person standing in front of the room. Next time around, they become the "tappers."

Note: The beauty of this game is that it is so *quiet*. Most children know how to play, and you can have a leader take over. It's a wonderful little filler for those extra five minutes when you need to transition to another activity. Because the game is so quiet, you will enjoy the peace!

- **Bingo Facts.**[1] This is a fun way to help students learn and recall weekly spelling words, vocabulary, math facts, geography (state capitals), science facts, or any other information. Before you start, fold a paper so that sixteen squares appear. Cut along the fold lines and number each square; put your squares into a container.

  Have students create a "bingo sheet" by folding a piece of notebook paper in half repeatedly until sixteen folded squares appear. Ask the students to write a small number in the upper right-hand corner of each square—*in random order*. Be sure to tell them to leave room within the square for writing an answer.

  Pick a square from your container one at a time, say the number of the square, and ask a question (e.g., a spelling word). Students must write the answer (e.g., the spelling word) in the square corresponding to the number you called. Whoever has completed a horizontal, vertical, or diagonal row—with correct answers—wins! Be sure to check for accuracy before declaring a winner. This is an easy game to play with all age groups (perfect for Grades 2–8).

---

1. A description of this game, along with other useful teaching tips, can be found at http://philville.com/sublessons.html.

What's the best strategy for getting a full-time job?

Dear Barbara,

I have been working for three years in the same school system. I would like to get a full-time job there, but I sense that it's not going to happen. I feel as if I'm invisible sometimes. There are days when I just don't feel respected.

How can I get the administration to notice and appreciate me?

Katherine in Kansas

Dear Katherine,

You are not alone. Many subs feel the same way, and you are correct in thinking that some people don't take subs seriously. If you have a feeling of isolation and a lack of respect, there are a few things you should do.

Always leave a complimentary note for the classroom teacher. Say you would love to sub in his or her class again. Try to strike up a conversation with the principal. Tell him or her what a nice group you are working with today. Mention that you admire the way the school is run. When you see the principal, make small talk, just as you would with any other teacher in the building. When an opportunity presents itself, be sure to mention that you are interested in obtaining a full-time position. Tell the administrators and other teachers about your goal.

If a long-term subbing position is offered to you, take it! These positions are the best route to a full-time job. Finally, if you can see that you are in a dead-end position, put your name on the subbing list in another school system. You never want to feel as if people are taking you for granted. Get a fresh start somewhere else, where subs are appreciated.

What if I suggest a game and the class has a different way of playing it?

Ask one child to explain their methods, and do it their way. There is no point in locking horns on this issue. Let the students continue to use their own class rules.

What should I do if there are "sore losers"?

In each class, there will be children who don't like to lose. Primary grade children have trouble understanding that they might lose or not get a turn. Try to set up rules and guidelines for this problem at the beginning of every game. Explain that "sore losers can ruin a game for all of us." By being proactive, you can eliminate hard feelings. Make a big issue about playing fairly and being mature when playing games. I tell the class that if they do not play like grown-ups, we will not continue the game.

If a child begins to act out because he has lost, pull him aside and have a talk. Ask him to be your helper until he settles down. Usually, peer pressure stops this kind of behavior because the other children want to keep playing.

Summary

Games can be used as a reward for good behavior and completed work. They are an excellent filler for those situations in which you have a bit of free time. The following guidelines will help:

- Try to make the games educational. They can be used to review material from the content areas. Use your teaching skills to adapt the games for educational purposes.
- Use classic games, but ask the students to teach you some of their own classroom games. You may even want to add these to your bag of tricks.
- Be aware that some children have trouble losing. Try to avoid these unpleasant scenes by setting clear guidelines.

Remember that if they are used properly, games can have solid educational benefits. They are an important part of your bag of tricks.

Helpers

As substitute teacher Laura Levy leafed through the plans for the day, she grimaced. Ten pages of notes were overwhelming. She was grateful for the detail, but a ten-page plan was just too much.

The classroom teacher had created an encyclopedia of forms, charts, pictures, and the like—all in an effort to manage the day. It probably worked for him, but for Laura it was too much. Laura found a paper plate with pictures of pizza, chicken nuggets, and a hot dog to be used for the lunch order; special clips for attendance; and a notebook to sign up for bathroom visits. There were steps and levels for managing behavior and reward charts everywhere. It was mind-boggling!

Breathe deeply, thought Laura, *you will get this figured out*. She was jolted out of her thoughts by the morning bell. Third graders began to enter the classroom.

A little girl with her hair in pigtails was the first to enter the room. She smiled at Laura and began to unload her backpack in an orderly manner. Laura studied her for a moment, looked at the seating chart, and decided that Brittany would make a perfect helper for the morning activities.

"Brittany?" said Laura in a soft voice. Other students were moving toward their seats.

The girl looked up. "That's me!"

"Can you give me some help with the attendance today?"

Brittany's face lit up. "Sure, I help Mr. Cardozo all the time!"

Laura smiled and thanked Brittany. Her new helper would assist in deciphering Mr. Cardozo's intricate morning routine. With her help, Laura would be able to execute his plans.

Like it or not, many things that happen in a classroom—taking attendance, doing the lunch count, processing tardy slips, or collecting money for a class trip, to name a few—are only peripherally connected to the curriculum. All of these "logistics" activities require that you follow a specific process and that you know the name of each student. As a sub, it's your job to complete each activity, but you'll need help. Students will be happy to assist you, but it's important to know how to pick a helper and how to manage the help you do receive. That's what this chapter is about.

How do I choose the trusted helper?

Choosing a special or trusted helper is an art, not a science. Therefore, there are no hard-and-fast rules for picking the perfect person. But there are personality types you might want to avoid:

- **The space cadet.** This child is always in dreamland, staring into space and living in his own world. He may be a very nice child, but as a helper, he could be a disaster.
- **The gabber.** This child may be a sweetheart, but she is incessantly communicating with her peers. She's more

concerned about having a conversation than participating in classroom activities.

- **The slob.** This child may be bright and loved by his peers, but his desk is a mess, his supplies are piled haphazardly, and litter sits on the floor around him. He might be anxious to help, but the end result could be a mess.

So, what should you look for in a helper? Sometimes it's the quiet child or the student who appears to be "nerdy." These children often have the best grasp of classroom logistics. At other times, it's the child who greets you with a warm smile and exhibits a sense of curiosity. It's likely that such a student will help you with enthusiasm and good humor. Occasionally it can be the potential "troublemaker." By keeping this child close and giving him or her responsibility and respect, you may actually eliminate potential problems downstream. Before you make your selection, check if there is a helper chart on the classroom bulletin board. The class may have assigned helpers for the week already.

Once you've chosen a candidate, ask her to come to your desk. Quietly ask if she would like to help you out today. Usually the answer will be yes, but if the student is not interested in the job, be sure to have a backup candidate.

Occasionally you will make a mistake and choose a student who decides to make a joke of helping you. If this happens, *immediately* ask the student to return to his seat and choose another helper. Your second choice will rarely exhibit the same behavior.

How do I get the helper started?

Once a student has agreed to assist you, begin immediately. Try to defer to the student's expertise in logistics matters. It bolsters the child's self-esteem and encourages him or her to do a good job. Consider the following conversation:

You: This is my first time in Mr. Blackman's [the classroom teacher] classroom, Alexis [your

helper]. So, I'll need your help with some things.
Are you ready?

Helper: Uh, huh.

You: How does Mr. Blackman take attendance in the
morning?

Helper: Well, he asks everyone to remain seated,
and he just takes attendance by calling out our
names. I think he marks it on a piece of paper
[the attendance form].

You: Okay, Alexis, I'll do that, and you stay up here
and tell me if I'm doing it correctly. You can help
me pronounce names, just in case I get stuck!
Also, I want you to make sure that the right
person answers when I call each name. Can you
do that for me?

Helper: Uh, huh. I will.

It's very important to assign tasks that are narrowly focused
and simple enough to ensure the helper's success.

Do I need to keep the same helper for the whole day?

It's a good idea to choose different students throughout the
day. You will need helpers to pass out papers, helpers to bring
notices to the office, door holders, and students to help you
clean up at the end of the day. You might need helpers during
recess or when students go to special classes or events.

Use as many children as you can, making sure to impart
a level of prestige to each child who helps. The class becomes
part of a team, and, unconsciously, the goal of the team is to
make your life easier.

What about class jobs?

Many classrooms have class jobs that are assigned by the
classroom teacher and are usually posted on the bulletin

How can I make some extra income?

Dear Barbara,

Is there a way that I can earn extra money while subbing? The pay is so bad, but I really want to teach. I know that subbing is the best way to prepare for my career and to make good contacts. But I can't survive on the unsteady, small paychecks.

Matthew in New York

Dear Matthew,

There are many things you can do to supplement your income while subbing. Here are a few suggestions that will keep you involved in teaching and provide you with extra income. Try tutoring. Tell the principal, reading specialist, chairman of the Math Department, and the guidance counselor that you are a qualified tutor. Have cards or brochures made up for distribution.

You can also check with the adult education department in your district. Teachers are needed for night school, General Education Development (GED) programs, and English for Speakers of Other Languages (ESOL) programs for recent immigrants. These part-time jobs are wonderful because they will give you practice teaching, look good on a résumé, and open doors for full-time employment, while leaving your days open for subbing jobs.

board. Teachers change these jobs weekly, typically each Friday. There are usually enough jobs for everyone in the class, ranging from line leader to the person who puts the trash can near the door. Make note of these jobs and do not assign informal helpers to them. If you do, you'll slight the permanent job holder and create problems within the classroom.

Is it a good idea to choose a "problem student" as my helper?

In general, this is recommended, but you must proceed with caution. For younger students, you should start slowly by asking for help on a specific small task. If things go well, you can increase the scope of the work to be performed. For older children, you must be subtle. They are sophisticated enough to perceive that you're trying to "buy them off" and may respond poorly. Your request for help should appear offhand and genuine. For middle schoolers, be aware that children who are perceived as the teacher's pet can be set up for ridicule. Again, subtlety is demanded in these situations.

If handled properly, this approach can enable you to control a difficult student by making him or her an ally rather than an adversary. If it goes well, use lots of praise to reinforce positive behavior.

What about the child who is a loner?

Unfortunately, children who are not accepted by their peers are sometimes rejected by the classroom teachers as well. These children are starved for attention and recognition. If you make an effort to take a special interest in a student like this, you will be rewarded with a good helper. More important, asking a "loner" to help you is a wonderful way to bring him or her into the fold.

What are the opportunities for me to choose helpers?

Whenever you choose a helper, you allow a child to cross a subtle boundary that separates teachers and students. As students cross this boundary as helpers, they become part of a team that is working toward the efficient operation of the classroom. (Of course, they don't perceive it that way, but it does happen.) It increases efficiency, enhances classroom management, and reduces the chaos that occurs when confusion abounds. Here are some opportunities to achieve these benefits:

- Taking attendance and lunch count
- Making trips to the office
- Taking another student to the nurse (in the primary grades)
- Passing out papers
- Assuming a leadership role when playing games
- Cleaning up at the end of the day
- Answering questions for you about material
- Finding items in the classroom
- Serving as door holders

As you go through a typical day in the classroom, it's likely you'll encounter many opportunities for helpers. These are really win-win situations. The students win through prestige and participation, and you win because your day will be easier.

Summary

Using classroom helpers is a wonderful way to empower students, improve their self-esteem, and make your day in the classroom much easier. Students know things about classroom logistics that you don't. Use them to help!

Consider the following guidelines when selecting and using helpers:

- Observe students early, and use your intuition to avoid those who might not be good helpers and choose those who would be.
- Keep each helper's task focused and relatively simple. Be sure to set the conditions that will make the helper succeed.
- Choosing a problem student as a helper must be done with caution, but it can successfully solve behavior problems.
- Choosing a loner as a helper does much to improve the child's self-esteem and classroom prestige.
- Virtually every classroom activity can be an opportunity for the selection of a helper.

When students help with classroom tasks, all of you are working as a team. A good sub knows how to choose helpers wisely, pairing students and tasks in an effort to make the students succeed and the classroom run more efficiently. An effective sub knows how to get students on his or her side, and helpers provide the best opportunity to achieve this goal.

Date:
Girls: 9
Boys: 8
Total: 17

Introducing Yourself

Elizabeth Heinrich had been a substitute teacher for less than a month when she was assigned an eighth-grade class in Prospector's Middle School in Deadwood, South Dakota. This class had a reputation as a "challenging group." As she entered the classroom, Elizabeth tried to overcome a feeling of mild panic, recognizing that she had to win the students over quickly.

In her past classroom assignments, Elizabeth had introduced herself briefly and moved on to attendance and early morning activities. But for this class, she sensed that a more personal approach was both necessary and essential. But what could she do?

Behind the teacher's desk was a large, grainy black-and-white photograph depicting gold rush prospectors, circa 1885. The school in which she was teaching had been named in honor of their exploits. She looked at the picture, and, suddenly, it hit her. She knew how to introduce herself.

"Good morning," she said with a smile to a class of noisy eighth graders. "My name is Mrs. Heinrich, and my great-great-grandfather was one of these men." She jerked her thumb backward toward the picture.

The classroom noise level dropped immediately.

"He's in the picture?" asked a boy in the second row. "He was a prospector during the gold rush?"

"He's not in the picture, but yes, he was a real-life prospector," said Elizabeth with a twinkle in her eye. She had engaged the class.

For the next ten minutes, she told stories about her great-great-grandfather during the gold rush, using all the dramatic skills she could muster. The students were spellbound. They asked questions and mentioned interesting family members of their own. A wonderful discussion followed. Elizabeth could feel a growing sense of trust and confidence.

The rest of the day went smoothly, and behavior problems were minimal. She was certain that the bonding that had occurred during her story, which was very real and from the heart, created respect.

In his bestselling book *Blink*, Malcolm Gladwell contends that human beings are particularly adept at making rapid, intuitive decisions based on very little hard information. Interestingly, those intuitive decisions are often correct. The instant in time when you introduce yourself to a classroom full of students is one of those "blink" moments. Your body language, your tone of voice, the confidence you project, and the words you use are all part of an image that helps the students decide what type of person you are and, unconsciously, how they will interact with you throughout the day.

You have little more than a "blink" to establish yourself, and that's why it's so important to introduce yourself properly to the class. In this chapter, I'll suggest how you can do it effectively.

What should I do as students begin entering the room?

Greet the students as soon as they walk in. If you're working in a primary grade, it's wonderful to greet them at the door with a warm "Good morning, how are you today?" Or, "I love that shirt!" Or, "Your hair is so pretty today." Or, "Those are great sneakers. Are they new?"

One or more students will ask who you are (if it's your first time in the classroom). As the students are entering the room, you might respond with, "I'll be teaching for Ms. X today. I'll tell you more about myself once everyone is here."

How should I introduce myself?

Once all students have arrived and it's time to start the day, take the time to tell students who you are. First, write your name on the board. Turn to face the class, making eye contact with as many children as possible, and say your name. Then get personal! Tell the class about yourself and your family. Talk about children, pets, your spouse, and any hobbies you enjoy. If you're a New England Patriots fan, let them know.

Be sure to describe any teaching experience that you have had. It gives you credibility. For example, "I was a first-grade teacher for many years. It's a real treat for me to work with sixth graders today. You guys are so capable and independent!"

After you introduce yourself, you have a decision to make. If the students seem blasé and disinterested (it does happen), move directly into the day's work. But if you feel that you've engaged the class well, you might want to keep the good feeling going by asking the students to introduce themselves.

"I'd like to learn something about each of you," you might say. "Tell me your name, but more important, tell me something about yourself, so I can get to know you better."

Be careful not to let these introductions run too long. When you sense you've spent enough time on the activity, stop and tell the students that you'll meet the rest of them throughout the day.

What's the best way to take students to an assembly?

Dear Barbara,

The last time I subbed, we had a student assembly. I wasn't sure how to proceed from the classroom to the auditorium, where we were supposed to sit, or what behavior standards were expected of the students. As a consequence, I was really confused and nervous. To make matters worse, my students behaved poorly, and I suspect it was because I was not the regular teacher.

If I can't control the students' behavior in a public setting, I look bad in front of the other teachers. Are there any tricks to ensuring good behavior during assemblies?

Carlene in Detroit

Dear Carlene,

There are specific things you can do to improve behavior for assemblies. Just as with all good teaching, you must be prepared and set clear expectations.

When you read your plans and see that an assembly is scheduled, call aside a special helper. Ask him or her what the normal routine is for proceeding to the auditorium and where your class should sit. If there is time, ask a grade partner these same questions for added insight. Ask what the subject matter will be. Now you'll have the information you need.

Tell the class in advance what time you'll be leaving for the assembly, and tell them what the content of the program will be. You might ask them what they already know on the topic as well as what new things they think they might learn.

Review your rules and expectations for assembly behavior. Tell your class that you expect them to walk quietly in line and that they must sit next to someone who will not "get them in trouble." Mention that you may find it necessary to change some seats if you see some people talking to one another.

Use proximity to help you monitor behavior. Use a special look or hand motion that you have explained earlier as a warning system. Finally, if someone is out of control, take that student off to the side and have that student sit near you and away from the others until he or she demonstrates the ability to return to the group.

This technique is effective because students will find it harder to act out and cause problems for you when they are aware that you know something about them and cared enough to ask.

I like to tell the children that I have two sons, their ages, and some cute little quirky things about each one. Just being a mom gives me credibility. If this is not the case for you, tell the students something interesting about your siblings, nieces, nephews, or even pets to accomplish the same goal.

I have a nephew who is (at the time of writing this book) on a Big East college basketball team. He is a dedicated athlete who has worked hard to get to his position. I love to tell students his story. It is inspiring and creates a fascination, especially for those students who aspire to be athletes.

I also like to tell stories about myself when I was their age. Children love to hear what life was like "back in the day." As a sub, you can create a real bond with the class by being an interesting, sharing individual. Give it a try!

Summary

You only get one chance at a first impression. When you introduce yourself to a classroom full of students, you lay the foundation for their interaction with you. The following guidelines are worth considering:

- Greet students individually as they walk into the classroom. Smile.
- Write your name on the board and then make eye contact with as many students as possible as you begin your introduction.
- Get personal; tell them something about yourself, your background, or even your family.
- If you feel a good vibe, ask them about themselves.

If you introduce yourself effectively, you're much less likely to have behavioral problems throughout the day.

Jokes: Using Humor

A faint smile crept across Scott Irwin's face as he surveyed the students in his history class. Every teenager's head was bent forward, arm cradling an exam book, writing furiously. *They'll do well on this exam*, he thought. Now in his fourth week of a long-term subbing position at East Ridge Middle School, Scott had worked hard to prepare them for the test.

Scott stretched and stood up. Out of the corner of his eye he noticed an unusual movement, nothing obvious, just slightly out of place. A young man named Enrique, sitting two rows from the rear of the classroom, had quickly changed positions, putting his left hand in his lap. Scott, an observant and experienced sub, suspected that the answers to the exam were written on Enrique's hand.

As Scott meandered slowly toward the back of the room, a few students glanced up and then returned to their exam books. He paused for a moment when he reached the second row from the rear. Enrique squirmed in his seat, tiny blue ink words clearly visible on his left hand.

Scott knew that there were a number of different ways he could handle this situation. He didn't say a word as he turned and walked to the front of the classroom. One or two students sensed something was up and glanced in his direction. Scott cleared his throat loudly—a few more students looked up. With a theatrical flourish, he reached into his desk drawer, removed a red pen, and walked back to Enrique's desk. At this point half the class was watching, not sure what was going on, but certain that something was up.

Scott leaned forward over Enrique's desk and smiled broadly. "Enrique," he said with enthusiasm, "nice work!"

Enrique's face reddened.

Now the entire class was engaged.

Scott made eye contact with a number of students, still smiling broadly. He returned his gaze to Enrique who now looked confused. "May I see your left hand?" he asked matter-of-factly.

Enrique groaned.

Scott took his red pen and wrote "100%" on Enrique's left hand. "I'm going to give you a grade of 100 here, Enrique," said Scott, pointing at Enrique's hand with his pen. "But I have to give you a 0 on your test paper."

Laughter cascaded across the classroom.

Rather than being confrontational, Scott Irwin used humor to correct a classroom situation, and, at the same time, he was able to keep the entire class on his side. Even Enrique had to smile. Mr. Irwin was a funny guy who knew how to keep his cool.

By defusing a serious breach of classroom protocol, Scott Irwin demonstrated a few important skills that every sub should learn. First, he taught the students that he was aware of their behavior, even when they might try to hide things. They learned that it was pretty hard to pull a fast one on him. Second, he used his sense of humor to demonstrate his leadership and "withitness." (See more on "withitness" in the

X-Ray Vision chapter.) Mr. Irwin was cool. Third, he became a "legend"—someone who commanded respect. The story of Enrique's hand would spread quickly, and, as a result, everyone would know that Scott Irwin was not someone to trifle with. Humor works!

How can I use my sense of humor in the primary grades?

Jenna Mathews began her day as a sub with a tearstained blouse, trying to console a six-year-old girl in her first-grade class. As the children entered the room, Jenna learned that two students had argued on the bus. Sarah came in crying uncontrollably. There was no way to calm her down. Jenna dried her tears, but the sobs continued, even when Jenna tried to distract her. This crying spell was escalating out of control.

The argument on the bus was over long ago, but the pain continued. Jenna knew that all the reasoning in the world would not make the crying stop. Because she was an experienced sub, Jenna Mathews began making very small crying sounds herself. Immediately Sarah quieted down and looked strangely at her sub. Ms. Mathews explained that if Sarah continued to cry, she would have to cry too since it was so sad to listen to those sobs. The more Ms. Mathews "cried," the bigger the smile grew on Sarah's face. Soon they were both laughing. Problem solved.

How do I know when humor will work?

When you need to lighten up a situation, a smile is your best tool. It diffuses tension and shows that you are in control. It takes confidence to use humor effectively, and confidence is the image you want to project.

But you have to feel comfortable using humor in the classroom. If this is not authentic for you, then you shouldn't even attempt it. But that doesn't mean you shouldn't smile. For many teachers, however, the children are an audience and the classroom is their stage. Sometimes you have to be a dramatic actor, and sometimes you need to be a comedian.

A successful teacher and high school basketball coach from New York City once told me that he started each day with a joke for his students. The jokes were usually pretty corny, but over time, he developed excellent comic timing and delivery. His students began looking forward to his morning jokes and would object if he started a day without one. A bond was formed.

Because of his sense of humor, virtually every student considered Coach a great guy. It was obvious that he was comfortable with himself and comfortable with the students in his classes. By making the effort to find jokes for them each day, he demonstrated that he cared. Instant respect!

How do I know if a joke is appropriate?

Obviously, you must be *very* sensitive to content. It is never appropriate to tell a joke that has racial, sexual, or gender-biased overtones—no matter how innocent it is or how many laughs it might get. Under no circumstance is it appropriate to tell a joke that indirectly ridicules a specific student or group of students. Never make a joke at the expense of a student. Stated bluntly, never tell a joke that you wouldn't want to see printed in the newspaper under your picture.

Certain jokes are appropriate only for specific grade levels. Students in primary grades, for instance, love riddles and silly rhymes. They like jokes that they can remember and repeat to siblings and parents. Ask students to tell jokes and riddles to the group. They love to take the stage, and I have found that students listen to their classmates more than they listen to the teacher. Here is a joke that I learned from a first grader:

Question: Where are pencils made?
Answer: In Pennsylvania

Jokes for middle school students can be more sophisticated. Ideally, the humor you use with middle schoolers should have some direct relationship to their world.

Regardless of the types of jokes you choose or your application of humor to everyday classroom events, it's important to

How can I be sure I won't lose my temper?

Dear Barbara,

I'm generally mild mannered, but every once in a while something sets me off and I lose it. Obviously, I never want that to happen in the classroom, but I came dangerously close this afternoon.

I was teaching middle school reading, working with students who struggle academically. I tried hard to keep them involved in the lesson, but it was obvious they weren't terribly interested in the work—especially when a sub was teaching them.

I simply could not hold their attention. As they began to act out, I began to become frustrated and then angry. At one point I yelled and then I pleaded. Even I could sense that I sounded pathetic!

How can I avoid losing my temper?

Adam in Los Angeles

Dear Adam,

Every sub has had days like yours. You are not alone, and you shouldn't be too hard on yourself. There are days when you just can't seem to gain control, no matter what you do.

Please remember one thing—no matter what happens in that room, no matter how angry you feel, do not lose your temper. Once you do, you are no longer in control. Be aware that you are the authority figure in the classroom and your actions set the tone for the entire day.

When classroom behavior begins to deteriorate, try to focus on the few students who are cooperating. Praise them. Change your voice intonation. Tell the class that when work is completed you have a fun activity planned.

Then try to isolate the source of disruption. Usually one or two students are the culprits. Rather than punishing the whole class, take aside the cause of the problem, look him right in the eye, and ask him to get to work now. Tell him this is his one and only warning. If he continues to act out, give him a referral or a detention or send him to the office with a note. This will show the others that you are serious. Sometimes you need to make an example of one student to get everyone's attention and to gain control.

be spontaneous. Humor and jokes bomb when they appear to be contrived or forced. Start out slowly and see how it goes.

It's also important to recognize that smiles must be earned, especially when you're dealing with middle school students. When you first meet a middle school class, a big smile might be misinterpreted by the students. As strange as it might seem, they may think of you as an easy mark—weak and insecure. Let students earn your smile. If you are particularly charmed by a comment or especially proud or touched by a special moment, let yourself smile to reward the situation.

Is it ever appropriate to use sarcasm rather than humor?

I'm against the use of sarcasm because it belittles the student and rarely accomplishes its intended goal. In many instances, students perceive a sarcastic remark as mean-spirited. However, some teachers find it to be effective for classroom management and use it effectively with older children.

Where can I find good jokes?

There are many books and websites with jokes that are appropriate for children and teenagers. Spend a few minutes visiting these websites:

- **enchantedlearning.com/subjects/dinosaurs/Dinojokes .html**—original dinosaur jokes
- **brownielocks.com/jokes.html**—jokes and riddles
- **kidhumor.glowport.com**—e-mails a joke a day
- **myhumor.org**—jokes for older students
- **jokesbykids.com**—jokes for and by kids

In addition, the following books will provide you with an excellent collection of jokes that can be used in the classroom:

- *Kids' Silliest Jokes* by Jacqueline Horsfall and Buck Jones (Sterling, 2003)
- *Knock, Knock! Who's There? My First Book of Knock Knock Jokes* by Tad Hills (Little Simon, 2000)
- *The Treasury of Clean Teenagers' Jokes* by Tal D. Bonham (Broadman and Holman, 1997)
- *1001 Animal Quacker Jokes* by Jasmine Birtles and David Mostyn (Constable and Robinson, 1998)

Remember, if it sounds like you're reciting a joke, it will bomb. Be spontaneous and tell the joke in the proper context. In addition to jokes you can acquire from the sources I've just mentioned, here are a few situations and ways you can use humor with good results:

- I knew a high school PE teacher who required his students to wear the school gym shirt/uniform each day. One day a young man came with a messy, torn shirt with holes in it. The PE teacher said, "I told you to wear the gym shirt, not a golf shirt."

    "I am NOT wearing a golf shirt," the student replied.

    "Yes, you are," said the teacher, "that shirt has 18 holes!"
- As part of a unit on first aid, a health teacher was teaching his students about poisons. With a straight face, he asked what they would do if a friend accidentally swallowed gasoline. He got some very astute answers. He then told the students that it actually happened to a student of his four years ago. The class asked, "What did you do?"

    "I had him run around the track until he ran out of gas."

And for younger students:

- What has four wheels and flies? A garbage truck
- What is a frog's favorite drink? Croaka-Cola

- Why can't your nose be twelve inches long? Because it would be a foot!
- Where do cows go on Saturday nights? To the mooovies
- Why didn't the skeleton go to the movies? He had no body to go with.

Summary

Humor can be one of your most important tools in the classroom. It can be used as a tension reliever, to defuse a difficult situation, or simply as a way to break up the day. The following guidelines will help you use humor effectively:

- Cultivate a few effective jokes for each grade level and use them when the context warrants.
- Be spontaneous when you use humor. Smile and laugh with the students.
- Always be certain that any joke you tell is appropriate for the age level and the audience.
- Never tell a joke that is offensive.
- Try not to be sarcastic, and never ridicule a student.

Using humor in the classroom is an art. It gives you an opportunity to add some laughter to the lives of your students. Practice, experiment, and have fun with it.

Kickball,
Physical Education,
and Other Specials

I n mid-September I received a call from the principal of an elementary school that housed all of the Kindergartens in a rural town in Connecticut.

"We have a part-time PE teacher who comes in for two hours each day to teach our Kindergarten children," the principal began. "She's going to be out for six weeks due to an unexpected illness requiring surgery. We're desperate for a sub, and we'd like you to fill in for her."

"You should know that I'm not much of an athlete," I admitted. The assignment was appealing because I knew I would have six weeks of work in one school. I hoped that my lack of athletic ability would not be a concern.

"Not a problem," replied the principal. "We know you'll do a fine job."

And so, my long-term subbing assignment began.

I immediately called a friend who was an elementary PE teacher, and she gave me some great ideas. I researched games for children online. I recalled games that I played as a child. I was ready.

On the first day of the assignment, I came to school in my gym teacher persona—shorts, a polo shirt, sneakers, a baseball cap, and a whistle—to give me what I thought was an authentic look.

As the kindergarteners ran into the gym (they never walk), they had no way of knowing that their new PE teacher wasn't an athlete. I wasn't worried. I had planned warm-up exercises, some dancing, and other appropriate activities. No problem.

A little boy ran up to me immediately. He had a big smile and the frenetic enthusiasm of a five-year-old. "Umm, hi. When are we going to play basketball?"

I panicked. Basketball? I wasn't even sure of the rules.

"What's your name?" I asked, stalling.

"Brandon."

"Well, Brandon, today we're going to play some other games."

Brandon frowned.

"You'll see, they'll be fun!" I said with enthusiasm.

"Okay," he said, slightly downtrodden, "but my dad wants me to learn how to dribble."

"I'm sure you will, Brandon," I said. *Just not in my class*, I thought.

During my six weeks as a PE teacher, I began each class with warm-up exercises, running, jumping, skipping, hopping, and simple drills using balls and equipment from the PE closet. I finished each class by playing my CD with songs such as *YMCA*, *The Chicken Dance*, *The Hokey Pokey*, and *The Macarena*. The children loved it, and so did I.

Brandon may not have learned how to play basketball during those six weeks, but he certainly would have been very comfortable at a wedding when the band played line dances!

Each of us has an educational specialty. Some teachers love writing, others enjoy history, some specialize in math. As a sub, you'll be no different. You'll have a favorite subject area. But as a sub, you'll need to be adaptable and willing to extend yourself when the need arises. If I had let my incompetence and insecurity as an athlete affect my decision to accept a job as a PE teacher, I would have missed out on an enjoyable long-term subbing assignment.

Being a sub for a "special" can be a challenge, but you also can count on an interesting day with plenty of variety. Students are always happy to be in your room because specials are a pleasant break from the normal academic day. The arts provide a much-needed creative outlet while the computer lab and media center enable students to explore the world of information. PE provides them with a way to burn off excess energy.

So don't be afraid to become a "specialist" for a day or a week or a month. You might find the experience rewarding in ways you did not imagine when you accepted the assignment.

Why are subs assigned for special teachers?

When students are sent to specials, classroom teachers get a well-deserved break. In most cases, the classroom teacher uses that break for planning. In other situations, the break might be used for a special meeting with administrators or parents. It might even be used to visit the bathroom! So when a specialist is absent and there is no sub, the classroom teacher is not happy.

What challenges will I face?

Teaching a special is different and will pose a number of unique challenges. Among the most common are:

- **You will see all the grade levels in one day.** This means that you will have to adjust your demeanor accordingly. With each grade level, you'll set a different tone and your activities will have to be age appropriate.
- **You will have each class for a short period of time.** This may present pacing issues, and it's important to plan the class well. But overall, it's a good thing. If the students present behavior problems, you only have to put up with them for an hour or less. And when things go smoothly, you'll be sad to see them go.
- **You will be expected to have some basic, general knowledge of the special area of interest that you are teaching.** Most specials provide sub plans that do not require any great skill level (often a video). However, I recommend that you have a few ideas for each special in case you need them for extra fill-ins. If you know about the assignment in advance, it's best to stop in and see the teacher the day before so that you can have advance knowledge of what you might be teaching.

What if I am asked to sub for the PE teacher?

The PE teacher will generally leave plans that require an easy game that the group is comfortable with. Some examples are kickball, soccer, field hockey, and volleyball.

A special helper can give you advice on the way things are "usually done." (See the Helpers chapter.) If the game requires a monitor or referee, I always appoint a student to help me with this. You may not be familiar with the rules, but your special helper will be.

If the students are cooperative and they finish the game early, they may ask for free, unstructured time. They may want to organize teams and play in small groups. Use your judgment here, and make it a reward. If anyone takes advantage of this, remove the offending student from the group for five minutes. Tell the other students that you will stop the free time *immediately* if they are not cooperative.

PE teachers are trained to see everything and to be acutely aware of potential safety issues. Be sure to make yourself familiar with the procedures for handling accidents, authorizing trips to the nurse (be sure to send a classmate with the injured student), and handling blood borne pathogens. A good sub is informed of these procedures beforehand, and the school district may have a safety orientation. However, it is up to you to be sure you get the information you'll need.

What if I am asked to sub for the art teacher?

Some of us can draw realistic portraits that result in *oohs* and *aahs* from everyone who sees them. Others have trouble drawing a good stick figure. The good news is that even the artistically impaired can sub effectively in an art class.

Most art teachers have special plans for subs. The projects require simple tools, usually crayons and paper for younger children and pencil sketching for older students. Regardless of the simplicity of the project, be sure to set guidelines at the beginning of each class. Explain the project clearly, define what the students are supposed to create, and establish a procedure for handing out and collecting supplies. Write all directions on the board.

But what if there is no sub plan? That's why I always keep a few how-to-draw books in my personal bag of tricks. For primary classes, I show the children how to make a cat, horse, or cartoon character. Using the simple steps shown in the book, I draw each step on the board and have the children follow my lead. When they are finished, they can color their pictures or make more. I encourage them to keep practicing until they master the technique. For older children, you might try one or more of these ideas:

- Have the students draw pictures of their rooms at home. See how many details they can remember. Then ask them to add some things that they wish they could have in their rooms.
- Bring in a print or painting done by a famous artist with a distinctive style (Georgia O'Keeffe, Vincent van Gogh, Norman Rockwell). Promote discussion about the

masterpiece. Why is it famous? Discuss brush stroke, lighting, and shadows. Using the artist's style, have the students try to create their own works of art.

- Have students create a CD cover for their favorite musical group.
- Ask students to design a cool pair of sneakers with a unique brand logo.
- Have students do a graphic design for their favorite website.

Students of every age tend to love art class. Everyone has a creative side, and you can help students expand their potential creativity.

What if I am asked to sub for the music teacher?

Each time I've subbed for music in elementary grades, I've been told to show a video of a famous musical such as *Peter and the Wolf* or a Disney classic. This might work well, but in some cases, the children have seen the video many times, and they become bored quickly.

As an alternative to the video approach, here are a few ideas to add to the typical music sub plans for elementary grades:

- Write the words to a patriotic song on the board. Discuss each line. Ask students to choose one line that has meaning for them and illustrate it with a drawing. One example is the line "From the mountains, to the prairies, to the oceans white with foam." If you have a CD player, play the song while the students are drawing.
- Play a CD from a popular Disney musical and have students draw a picture of their favorite character or scene.
- Have children work in pairs or work alone to write a rap song about their school. Have them perform the song at the end of the period.
- Create rhythm patterns—you clap a rhythm and students copy it. Make the rhythm more complex each time.

Finally, ask a talented student to lead. Repeat until all students have a turn to lead.

- Clap your name—have students say their first and last names and then clap the syllables to make a rhythm.
- Have students choose their favorite breakfast cereal and write a jingle for a TV commercial for it. They can present their jingles to the class.
- If you have time in advance, make up a word search with musical terms such as *treble, bass, clef, piano, trumpet, orchestra, soprano, alto, tenor,* and *band.*

What if I am asked to sub in the Media Center?

The Media Center is the place where the school's library books are located. It also houses music and video players and other audiovisual equipment. Educational tapes, CDs, DVDs, and other digital media are also stored in the Media Center. It is here that resources for teachers are plentiful. There is usually a paraprofessional or a parent volunteer to handle book returns. He or she will know the routine and can help you with the administrative details.

The typical routine for a Media Center sub is first to allow the students time to return an old book and choose a new book to borrow for the week. After this has been accomplished (toward the middle of the period), ask the children to sit together in a designated area (ask your special helper where that is) and read a story to the class. If you are left with extra time, the children may read silently or discuss the story that you have just read.

What if I'm asked to sub in the computer lab?

Every sub should have at least a rudimentary understanding of basic computer operations and interaction. If you have specific knowledge of Windows or Macintosh application software, all the better. On the other hand, if you're computer illiterate, you have some work to do. It's time for you to correct that problem.

What should I wear?

Dear Barbara,

I find it difficult to decide what to wear the morning of a subbing job. One day I was told that I would be teaching middle school science. I put on a knee-length skirt, white blouse, and high heels, which was very appropriate for my given assignment. I knew that dressing professionally would help me earn respect.

When I got to the office, the assistant principal told me that there had been a change and I would be the PE teacher for the day. Help!

Given the way I was dressed, I was very uncomfortable and looked ridiculous. I had to take off my shoes and walk around barefoot in the gym for the last period because my feet hurt so much.

Any suggestions?

Diana in Connecticut

Dear Diana,

You were correct in your choice of clothing for middle school science. A professional look goes a long way in creating an appropriate image and gaining respect. But as a sub, you must be ready for anything.

Keep "emergency" clothing in the trunk of your car. A pair of sneakers, a whistle, a knit shirt with a collar, and shorts or casual slacks will always work if you need to be a PE teacher for a day or if you are suddenly assigned to go on a field trip.

Your comfort is important. If you plan to wear high heels, put a pair of flats in your bag of tricks for the end of the day. Keep a sweater in your car in case the classroom is cold.

But remember that casual clothes are only appropriate when the assignment dictates them. Always dress like a professional. It does wonders for your sense of confidence.

When you sub in the computer lab, it's likely that the students will know far more about their computing environment than you will. This can make your life easy, if you choose your assistant wisely. It's very important to select a special helper who can assist you as you manage the lab. If possible, ask another teacher for a recommendation. Virtually every school has a "computer genius" student who will be more than happy to help.

It's likely that you'll be given plans for each class that visits the lab. In most cases, students will be working on a project and will continue with work from the last session. Sometimes students work on presentations or research projects. Computer graphics or yearbook entries may be on the agenda. Your job is to circulate around the room to monitor students' activities, ensuring that project work is being done correctly and that students are not surfing inappropriate websites or playing unauthorized computer games.

When students complete their activities for the day, they are usually allowed to play educational games or visit authorized websites. Use this option as a reward for good behavior.

Summary

When you are asked to sub for a "special" class, be prepared for a very different type of day. You'll be in contact with each class of students for only one period, so that even if a group is difficult the students will leave your room relatively quickly. The following guidelines will help you get the most out of this type of subbing assignment:

- Take the time to understand any special requirements. Will you need special clothing, materials, or equipment? Be sure you have whatever you need before students arrive.
- Find a special helper to assist you in understanding the particular routines of the class.

- Be sure to circulate and check up on inappropriate behaviors. Make yourself aware of safety precautions that lend themselves to these classes.
- Have a few extra lessons in mind, in case children finish early.

In most cases, subbing for specials is actually easier than classroom teaching. Students are happy to be there because specials break up the day and lack the stress of academic subjects.

Long-Term Subbing

I t was ten minutes before dismissal, and Ian Michael was feeling pretty good. After three days of subbing in Ms. Iola's sixth-grade classroom, he knew the names of all the students. He executed the morning routine flawlessly—attendance, lunch count, reciting the Pledge of Allegiance, and journal writing were a piece of cake. He understood how to maintain a busy daily schedule. Most important, the students liked and respected him. Real teaching was happening.

A little girl entered the classroom with a note. Ian read it and wondered why Mrs. Anderson, the school's principal, wanted to see him. After the class was dismissed, he walked down to the administrative offices and knocked on Claudine Anderson's door. She looked up and said, "Hi, Mr. Michael. Your day went well?"

Ian smiled, "Yes, it did. You wanted to see me?"

Mrs. Anderson thought for a moment. "Did you know that Ms. Iola will be out for six weeks?"

Ian shook his head. "I didn't. I hope it's not anything too serious?"

Mrs. Anderson shrugged her shoulders. "Well, she's having knee surgery and she'll be down for a while. We'd like you to take over her classroom for the duration. We'll pay you at a per diem rate."

Ian's eyes widened. A long-term assignment was perfect—better pay, stability, just like a full-time position. No surprises, no panic, no wondering what kind of plans would be left for him. He already knew the students and the routine.

Ian nodded. "I'd be happy to."

As Ian walked to his car, he realized that he now had full responsibility for the long-term education of the class. He smiled.

Once you've accepted a long-term subbing assignment, you'll need curriculum guidance, suggestions for grading papers and administering tests, and guidelines for many other day-to-day activities. I recommend that you try to contact the regular classroom teacher and schedule a face-to-face meeting (health or other scheduling variables permitting). Together, the two of you should map out a one-week plan. After the first week, you will be able to continue on your own, with limited guidance. During the longer term, you should work closely with your grade partner. But remember, you're now a long-term sub, and you will be able to put your imprint on the curriculum and the class.

How is long-term subbing different from day-to-day subbing?

Being offered a long-term subbing position is an honor. You have proven that you are reliable and capable. The faculty welcomes you, and, for a time, you will have a taste of what it would be like to have your own classroom. That's the good news.

But you'll also have increased responsibilities. You'll have to create your own lesson plans, and, at the same time, be certain to present all material prescribed by the curriculum for your grade level. To accomplish this, it's essential to confer with your grade partner.

In addition to planning and classroom scheduling, you'll also have responsibility for parental communication. If your long-term subbing assignment will span a number of months, it's a good idea to write a note to the parents, introducing yourself and assuring them that their children's learning will continue as normal. Before you do this, however, I suggest that you get guidance (and if necessary) permission from the principal.

On a day-to-day basis, you'll have responsibility for writing newsletters to parents, developing personalized notes that address a specific child's progress, and other forms of school-to-home communication. I cannot overemphasize the importance of checking spelling and grammar in all such communications. In fact, it's a good idea to have someone else proofread any document that is to be sent home.

Every teacher has responsibility for in-school paperwork (e.g., forms, reports, lists). Be sure you understand what your responsibilities are and complete all paperwork in a timely manner. Although teaching must take priority, a lax attitude about paperwork will not serve you well when administrators and other teachers evaluate your work.

You must be aware of the special needs children in your classroom. Some students may have an *Individual Education Plan* (IEP). This plan will indicate any special accommodations that should be made for the child. For example, it may state that the child needs extra time when taking tests, may need a quiet place to work, or may have modifications for homework assignments.

In addition to students with IEPs, some students may have a *behavior modification plan*. This plan defines a strategy for modifying a student's inappropriate or disruptive behavior. The plan often defines a series of rewards (e.g., stickers, positive note sent to parents) that are distributed throughout the day when the student meets predefined behavioral goals. For example, a student might receive a reward for good morning behavior, for good behavior during recess, for good behavior at lunch, and for good afternoon behavior. In general, the behavior modification plan may be nothing more than a white index card that is taped to a student's desk or inserted into the child's daily planner.

Will students accept me as their "regular" teacher?

If you follow the guidelines I've discussed in other chapters and set the tone of caring and confidence, there is no reason why the students will not embrace you as their own. But remember, it's likely that the students will be upset about losing their teacher for a long period. And they may worry about their teacher's health and well-being.

Recall the anecdote about Ian Michael at the beginning of this chapter. The day after he was offered the long-term assignment, Ian addressed the issue with his class.

"Some of you may not know that Ms. Iola will be out for about six weeks," he said, after the morning activities. "I'll be your teacher until she returns."

One child blurted, "That's because she's getting an operation on her leg, right?"

"That's right," said Michael, "but you should know that everything will be fine. I'll be talking with Ms. Iola often. She misses you and asked me to tell you that she's thinking of you."

A brown-haired, bespectacled girl toward the back of the room asked, "Will we do stuff exactly the same way Ms. Iola did?"

"We'll try," responded Michael, "but we'll also do some new things that I think will be fun. Just remember, we have lots of learning to do, and we want to give Ms. Iola a good report. Right?"

Heads nodded as the class waited for their new teacher to start the day.

Is there ever a situation in which I should turn down a long-term assignment?

As I've already mentioned, you should generally accept a long-term subbing assignment, particularly if you are trying to land a full-time position. However, if you're asked to accept a long-term assignment in a subject area that is foreign to you (this will probably only happen if the principal is desperate), you may want to think long and hard before accepting the position. For example, many of us are mathematically challenged. We know and can teach the basics, but doing a geometric proof may be a struggle. If you fall into that category, and you're offered a long-term assignment in a middle or high school math class, you might want to decline. In the Kickball, Physical Education, and Other Specials chapter, I discuss the special requirements for subs who must teach "specials."

I would advise you to do a little research on the makeup and disposition of the class before you accept the long-term position. If the class in question is a complete unknown to you, ask to sit in on the group one day. Be sure that you will be comfortable with the age group and subject matter. There are times when a group has had a series of subs who just couldn't handle them. You do not want to put yourself into this position unless you are very strong and ready for a challenge.

Can I put my own imprint on the class?

As a long-term substitute teacher, you have been entrusted with someone else's classroom. As a caretaker, you should try to maintain the same classroom culture—as long as it works for you. After all, the regular classroom teacher will return, and it's your job to ensure that his or her transition back into the classroom goes as smoothly as possible.

But this doesn't mean that you can't be innovative and allow your teaching personality to shine through. Feel free to create your own class projects, if they complement the curriculum and enhance learning. For example, during his tenure in Ms. Iola's classroom, Ian Michael decided to create a class news-

What if students say, "We like you better"?

Dear Barbara,

Sometimes when I sub, the children confide in me that they like me better than their own teacher. I feel flattered, but I'm also uneasy about it. In some classrooms, they tell me that their teacher yells all the time.

I have two questions. How should I react to the comment about liking me better than the regular teacher? Do you think I should tell the principal about the teacher who yells all the time?

Ken in New Jersey

Dear Ken,

Students often like a sub better than their regular teacher. After all, if you do a good job and are kind to the children, you're a novelty. Unlike the regular teacher, you don't have to deal with the day-to-day stresses of grading, record keeping, parent conferences, and the daily challenges that students bring.

When you are told that you are liked more than Ms. X, thank the students, but explain that they have an excellent teacher and you admire Ms. X very much. Ms. X is responsible for their daily education, so she needs to be more serious sometimes. But you know that Ms. X is very proud of her class.

As far as reporting student comments about their regular teacher to the principal—absolutely not! You must never indulge in gossip like this. It is very unprofessional, and frankly, it's none of your business. The principal is well aware of the strengths and weaknesses of his or her faculty. The principal doesn't need your input in this instance, and it will reflect poorly on you if you provide it.

paper. He divided the class into groups, and they each had a role. He assigned committees for an editorial staff, an advice column, a puzzle page, an advertising section, and so on. The paper was "published" and sent home. Parents loved it.

One parent called the principal to praise the newspaper and the other work that Mr. Michael had done. When his time as a long-term sub concluded, Ian was asked to stay on and take a fifth-grade position that had opened up on a permanent basis.

Summary

A long-term subbing position will provide you with a clear opportunity to impress school administrators, which may ultimately lead to a full-time teaching position. There is no better way to test the waters. You'll learn all about the culture of the school, the faculty, and your comfort with a particular grade level. To be successful as a long-term sub, remember these guidelines:

- It is your job to reassure students who may be worried about their regular classroom teacher. Be sure to tell them that learning will proceed as normal and that their teacher will return when he or she is able.
- Students will respond well as long as you set a caring and confident tone. Follow guidelines provided in other chapters and you'll do fine.
- Be sure to budget time for planning. Consult with colleagues if you have questions or need guidance.
- Be sure to keep up with all parent communication, such as newsletters, and all required paperwork. Communication with parents and school administrators is an essential part of any teaching job.
- Put your own imprint on the class, but try to maintain the same classroom culture. That way the regular teacher's re-entry will be smooth.

If you've been offered a long-term subbing assignment, you've been given a potentially career altering opportunity. So if the opportunity opens up for you, seize the day!

Mentors

Pam Dawson was in the second week of a long-term subbing assignment at Buena Vista Elementary School. She
got along well with her students and seemed to be doing
okay when she presented her lessons, but the classroom just
didn't run very smoothly. In fact, things sometimes got a bit
chaotic.

Pam noticed that the fifth-grade teacher in the room next
door, Luisa Esposito, had the gift of organization. As a result,
her classroom ran like a finely oiled machine. Luisa was
friendly, and one day in the teacher lounge, Pam got up the
courage to ask for help.

"Luisa," Pam said shyly, "you've got such good control in
your class. Everybody seems to know exactly what to do. How
do you do it?"

Luisa smiled. "It's really not that hard. From the first day of school, I assign each of my students a job, teach them exactly how I want it done, and then reinforce good work with a lot of praise."

"So every child has a job?" asked Pam.

"Just about," Luisa responded. "One student has responsibility for taking attendance and another for passing out papers. A rotating group is assigned cleanup at the end of the day. I try not to remind them to do these things. I *expect* that the work will be done and the students get the idea. In fact, the kids like their jobs, and I'm sure they'd be upset if I took them away."

"So each child has one job for the entire year?" Pam asked.

"No, I rotate the jobs weekly. It keeps things fresh, and the children have an opportunity to try different jobs."

Pam thought a moment and then shrugged. "You know, I never hear you yell. How do you do that?"

Luisa smiled again. She enjoyed playing the role of mentor. "I turn off the lights."

"Huh?"

"If the children are getting noisy, I just turn off the lights— it's a signal for absolute quiet. That's why I almost never have to raise my voice."

Pam frowned. "But there must be some times when the students are uncooperative."

"We have a rule in my classroom," said Luisa. "If the students take time away from my teaching, I take time away from their free time. All I do is put a check on the board. They know, and it works like a charm."

"And the children seem to really adore you!" Pam couldn't help giving the compliment.

"We try to love one another," said Luisa. "It's the best part of the job."

Many subs are shy about asking for help. They tend to avoid requesting guidance because they don't want to look incompetent. But making serious mistakes can make you look bad, and getting good answers to good questions helps you avoid mistakes. The reality is that asking questions is one of the best ways to learn how to be a better teacher.

So don't be shy about looking for a mentor or at least a seasoned teacher who can guide you through rough spots. Most teachers are flattered when asked for help and can provide you with priceless tips that will make you a better teacher.

How can I ask other teachers for advice?

It's usually a good idea to begin the conversation with a compliment, follow with a self-deprecating or self-effacing statement, and conclude with a question. A few examples:

> *"It's amazing. Your students are so well behaved. I never hear a peep from your room. Sometimes I have a hard time getting my students to behave. How do you do it?"*

Or

> *"That's a really beautiful bulletin board. It must have taken a lot of planning. I'm sort of a klutz when it comes to art projects, but I know how important bulletin boards are. Do you have any pointers for the art-impaired?"*

Or

> *"Everything in your room is so well-organized, the students seem to know what you want them to do before you even ask. My room works okay, but it can get chaotic now and then. How do you get everyone to perform their jobs so effectively?"*

Everyone likes to be complimented. It's a sign of recognition and respect, and it almost always elicits a smile. People are rarely threatened by those who are honest about their own failings. That's why it's a good idea to follow a compliment with a self-effacing statement. Once you've set the stage, the potential mentor will be ready for your question.

I once had a long-term subbing assignment in sixth grade, and I was amazed at the way my grade partner, Andrew McDowell, was able to quiet his students with just a "look." I decided to ask him about it.

"Andy," I said one morning before school, "that 'look' of yours is magic! It quiets the kids down in an instant. I've tried soundless warnings, but they don't work very well for me. How do you get your 'look' to work so well?"

He laughed and explained that years ago, he developed a classroom management system that included a warning followed by consequences. Never two warnings, only one, and never weak consequences, only something that would be unpleasant. He explained to his students that his "look" was the only warning they would receive. If the "look" didn't achieve the desired result, there would be consequences. And his students learned (the hard way!) that the consequences would not be pleasant.

Your colleagues will be happy to share their knowledge with you. Because you are the sub, they know that you are not as experienced as they are. If you tell them that you would like to have your own classroom one day, they'll enjoy showing you how they do things. You have a marvelous resource right at your fingertips.

Should I ask an administrator for advice?

In general, an administrator will not become your mentor, but he or she can become an important sponsor if a long-term subbing position opens up or if there is a full-time position available at the school. In most cases, questions directed toward the principal and vice principal have to do with school procedures and protocols. However, almost all principals are experienced educators themselves, and they can provide useful advice if you encounter a teaching-related problem. They will remember that you cared enough to want to improve. Just be sure that you don't pester this busy person.

What should I do when students finish class assignments early?

Dear Barbara,

I seem to have a continuing problem in middle school classes. The regular teacher leaves work that the students are supposed to complete within a given time period. Some of the students rush through the work haphazardly. Then they start talking. When I ask them to stop, they say they have completed the assignment and have nothing to do.

In almost every instance, the perpetrators have not done a good job on the assignment. It's my feeling that some students don't want to work, they'd rather socialize.

I don't want to give out more work, but I need to keep them busy so they don't bother the serious students.

I am lost on this issue. Any ideas?

Jessica in Miami

Dear Jessica,

All teachers—not just subs—are challenged by this problem. Our students all have different learning styles and pace themselves differently. In addition, they have varying levels of interest in any given assignment. Some are neat, careful, and conscientious. Others rush through their work in an uncaring manner.

If a student says, "I'm finished," first check the work to be sure that it's correct and complete. If you are satisfied, go to your bag of tricks and choose from the extra material you have in there for the early finishers.

To stock up on the extra material, go online and print out age-appropriate material that will challenge the early finishers and still be "fun." Make several copies. For example, for younger children be sure to have word finds and other puzzles on hand. Some can be challenging, others easy. Hand out the extra work as needed.

You should provide a few choices so that the extra work doesn't feel like a punishment. Some students may say they prefer to continue working on the original assignment, which is fine!

As an alternative to handouts, you can write an assignment on the board for early finishers. You might post a question that you want them

(continued)

to respond to. It could be a list of vocabulary words to look up and use in sentences. You might have some brainteasers to work on quietly.

The trick is to have students on task at all times. You and the students will have a better day when everyone is busy.

Similar to the principal, other administrative staff may not have time to mentor you, but they can provide targeted advice in their area of expertise. For example, the school guidance counselor is an excellent resource if you have a student who has emotional issues. The guidance counselor will be able to tell you the most effective way of dealing with that student.

Summary

As a sub, you're usually on your own, but you will find colleagues who are happy to share their knowledge with you. When you find an experienced teacher whom you respect, have the courage to ask the right questions. You may acquire a mentor who can guide you through rough spots and provide advice that will help you be a much better teacher. Asking for help is easy, if you follow these guidelines:

- Don't think that asking questions will make you look incompetent. Good questions help you become a better teacher.
- Not every experienced teacher wants to be a mentor, but every experienced teacher will share knowledge if you approach him or her in the right way. Remember that good teachers love to teach, and they'll be more than happy to teach you.
- To get help, first give a compliment, be self-effacing, and then ask a relevant question. By complimenting a teacher,

you have shown interest in his or her work, and by being self-effacing, you demonstrate that you're not about to judge his or her advice.

- Administrators and staff can provide you with help, if you target your questions to their specialty. Just be sure that you recognize that administrators have many responsibilities and may not always have the time to answer multiple questions.

Don't be shy. People are flattered when asked for advice. Some will be happy to take you under their wing and serve as your mentor. You'll make a professional friend and become a more effective educator at the same time.

Names

"How do you do it?" asked Matt Davidson, a recent college graduate who had been subbing in Amity Center School for a few weeks.

Art teacher Anna Nuyen smiled and shrugged. "Years of experience, I guess."

Matt was incredulous. "But you see more than three hundred children every week—Kindergarten through Grade 6—and you remember their names! I noticed you don't use name tags, do you?"

"No."

"Then you must have a hidden name chart of some kind, right?"

Anna laughed. "Nah, my hands are too full of paint and glue to keep a seating chart."

"Then how?"

Anna thought for a moment. "It wasn't that easy for me at the beginning of my career. I use some tricks, actually. By now, I seem to have a knack for it."

Earlier in this book, I emphasized how important it is to know your students' names (and to learn something about each one of them). But how do you remember the names of all those children? In this chapter we'll examine how you can remember your students' names and review why it's so important.

Why is it important to learn my students' names?

Learning a student's name and using it establishes an instant connection. It shows that you care enough about a child to learn his or her name and that you are obviously an experienced and capable teacher. A student feels valued if a teacher calls him or her by name. At some subliminal level, the child feels closer to you and will almost always respond more readily to your requests.

There is almost a magical aura that surrounds a substitute teacher who can learn the name of every student before the end of the first day in class. The students know it's not easy to do that, and they are impressed with you. That's never a bad thing.

Will there be a seating chart or name cards?

The short answer is: there should be, but don't count on it. Principals often require teachers to leave a seating chart in a folder for substitutes. However, teachers tend to change seats often and don't always remember to update the seating chart. You shouldn't rely on its accuracy without other verification. To verify the seating chart, ask a special helper to assist you.

Most primary grade teachers keep large name cards on the children's desks. However, these cards rip and are often lost by mid-year. When I subbed and there were no name cards on the desks, I had the students fold notebook paper in thirds. Then I had them write their names on the papers and stand them up. If there was time, I asked them to decorate their name cards in a manner that described their interests. For instance, I told them that if they loved music, they could decorate their card with musical notes. I often made a sample to show them.

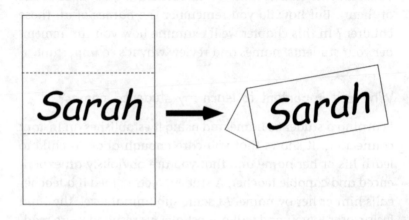

What should I do if I can't pronounce a student's name?

Mispronouncing a name is guaranteed to cause disruption, laughter, and embarrassment. When you are not sure of a name while you're taking attendance or teaching a lesson, there are two things you can do:

1. Quietly walk over to that student and ask him or her to help you learn how to say his or her name.
2. Ask a helper to go over the roster of student names with you before class begins. Your helper can teach you the proper way to address the students whose names might be foreign or unusual to you.

If you encounter a difficult name on a written list and can't exercise either of these options, you might say, "I'm not quite sure how to pronounce this name. I'll spell it, and you tell me how to say it properly."

Is there a better approach than yelling?

Dear Barbara,

I hate to yell, but sometimes it's the only way to get a class to listen to me. Sometimes a few students will stop and listen. Then they tell the others to be quiet, but in a loud voice! Now that they are "shushing" the others, the noise level grows even more intolerable.

What is the best way to get the class to quiet down so that I can give directions? I find it very frustrating when I have to waste five minutes before anyone listens. I know there must be a better way.

Samantha in Arizona

Dear Samantha,

The first thing I would do is ask your special helper to tell you the normal way of getting the class to quiet down. What does their teacher do? For younger children it might be flicking the lights, ringing a bell, or counting with a hand signal. Try using the normal method.

If you find that normal methods are ineffective, you might try telling the class that you have your own "special way" for asking the class to quiet down, just for use today. Make it a novelty and praise those who follow your technique.

I would recommend a special signal, such as five fingers in the air and counting backward. But—and here's the important part—use a very soft voice, count slowly, and once you have quiet, pause for effect and begin giving your directions in the same very soft voice. Thank the students for following directions, and proceed with your lesson.

Are there any tricks for remembering names?

Trying to remember the names of a classroom full of children may seem overwhelming for a new substitute teacher. But there are tricks that can help you.

- **Repeat the name immediately after you learn it.** Say "Hi, Marcus, nice to meet you."
- **When students are doing written work, walk around the room and look at their papers.** Compliment a student by name, while reading the name at the top of the paper. I have found this trick to be extremely effective.
- **When you want to praise a student's answer to a question, always praise using his name.** This will reinforce the name in your memory and will make the student feel that you respect him enough to remember his name.
- **Try to remember both the first and last names.** Believe it or not, remembering both is often easier than trying to memorize only the first name. One reinforces the other in your memory, and besides, sometimes the last name is easier to remember and will become a key for you to retrieve the first name.
- **Have the students introduce themselves using one adjective with the same letter as their first name,** such as Shy Shamika, Strong Sal, or Lively Larry.
- **Write the name in a notebook, and then write a short description of the student.** Define a code word for the student or provide a descriptive adjective starting with the same letter as the student's name. If you forget a student's name, try to picture the page in the notebook and visualize the written name.
- **Associate the student with a famous person or relative with the same name.** For example, Alex has a mischievous smile just like my nephew Alex. Tom is a real charmer, just like Tom Cruise.
- **Imagine the child with his or her name written across the forehead.**
- **Work out a little code word or song title.** If Rhonda is helpful in class, think about the song "Help Me, Rhonda."
- **If you see a past student in the hallways, be sure to greet her by name.** That student will be honored that you remembered her name outside of class and will be a good ally for you the next time you sub in her classroom.

It's best to use a combination of these tricks, but most important, you have to expend some effort. Learning your students' names quickly and accurately takes work, but the rewards make the effort worthwhile.

Is it possible to remember the names of a whole class in just one day?

Don't expect too much from yourself. Try to remember three or four names per class, adding three or four more each day. Even if you know only a few names at the end of the first day, you've established a solid foundation and have made connections with some of the students.

Ironically, we tend to remember the names of challenging students first. I suppose that's just a survival instinct among teachers! But don't forget about the quiet child. Learn his or her name as well.

Summary

Learning your students' names allows you to establish a quick connection with them. This can only help in establishing your credibility as a sub and will make classroom management much easier. To make learning names easier, follow these guidelines:

- Don't rely on the seating chart in the sub folder without checking it first. It may be accurate, but it's likely that the classroom teacher has changed seating assignments and not updated the chart. Verify the chart before you use it.
- Have the students (in lower grades) make name cards for their desks. It's a good idea to have them decorate the cards with something they like. The decorations will help you to remember the names.
- Use one or more of the memorization tricks discussed in this chapter. Choose the trick(s) that best matches your personal style of learning.

• Recognize that you won't know everyone's name by the end of the first day. But learning even three or four names each day is a good start.

The investment of time you make to learn your students' names will pay dividends in better classroom communication and improved classroom control.

Observe

Holly Stern was an education major who had finished her junior year at the local university. To earn extra money and to get some real teaching experience, she decided to sub at Davenport Elementary for the remainder of the school year.

Holly received a call from the sub coordinator three days after completing her paperwork at the school board office. As she dressed for her first day as a sub, she began to panic. *What do I do?* she thought while applying her makeup.

Her mother was in the kitchen when Holly came downstairs and offered her some toast and coffee before Holly left for her first day at school.

"I'm kind of nervous about this, Mom," Holly said as she sat at the kitchen table.

"Why, honey? You've had plenty of ed courses at the university. You said they are really good. And your grades are excellent!"

"I know, Mom. But, well, people tell me the real world is a little different."

"That it is," her mother smiled. "You know what you have to do, right?"

"What?"

"Look, listen, and learn, Holly."

Holly remembered her mother's words as she walked into Ms. Andrew's third-grade classroom. The room had a small library with cozy pillows and curtains. A behavior management system was clearly displayed. Ms. Andrews used a traffic light and clothespins with the students' names. Everyone started the day on the green light and would be moved to yellow and red if they misbehaved. The classroom rules were posted in cheerful primary colors for all to see.

Wow, thought Holly, *this stuff is great. I can use it when I get my own classroom.*

Holly sat in the teacher's chair and studied the materials on top of the desk. Ms. Andrew's lesson plans were thorough and easily understood. All Teacher's Guides were neatly displayed on the teacher's desk. Worksheets were organized by colors for each day of the week. The morning began with a journal entry, a math problem of the day, and daily oral language.

This classroom has all the characteristics of the perfect classroom that I learned about in my classes in the Education Department, thought Holly.

Luckily, Holly had just purchased a cell phone with a camera. She started taking pictures of the bulletin boards, library, and the desk setup so that she would remember as much as she could and reproduce it when she finally graduated and was ready to set up her own room. She looked and learned!

Look, listen, and learn—very good advice for even the most seasoned substitute teacher, and a crucial guideline for those of you who are just starting out. Someone once said that half of success is showing up. I contend that the other half is just paying attention. *Observation* is another way of saying the same thing.

How can I get the most out of my subbing experience?

Every day you walk into a classroom—look, listen, and learn. By applying the powers of observation, you'll walk away from your subbing experience with ideas that you can reuse in other classrooms and with other students. I recommend that you keep a spiral notebook in your bag of tricks. When you observe a good idea, write it down.

And don't confine yourself to observing only full-time classroom teachers. You can learn many tricks of the trade by observing other experienced subs.

You might argue that you don't have time to observe other teachers because you have a classroom of students to teach. That's true! So do the next best thing—ask questions. If you're a new sub, don't be afraid to ask more experienced full-time teachers and subs for ideas. If an idea works, it can become part of your repertoire. And if it doesn't work out for you, it's only one day and you'll know not to repeat it again.

What can I learn by observing students?

You'll be amazed at how much you can learn from students. As I mentioned in the Helpers chapter, students provide a wealth of knowledge about how things are done in the school and in the classroom. Ask students what methods are used to line up or to get students' attention. You will see which ones are effective and work with your individual personality.

In addition, students can often provide you with excellent ideas for "filler" activities and games. In fact, most of the classroom games that I use were taught to me by students. I was sure to ask them what they like to do when there is some extra time. Students love to teach a sub something new. Why not allow them to feel as if they are helping you?

Let's say you have fifteen minutes to fill before the students go to lunch. Here's how the interaction with your class might proceed:

"Let's do something special before we go to lunch," you say with enthusiasm.

What should I do when a student says, "I don't get it"?

Dear Barbara,

I find it very frustrating to have to repeat directions over and over again. No matter how clearly I explain things, there are always a handful of students who never pay attention. They expect me to repeat the directions, just for them. I am tired of the dreaded words, "I don't get it"!

I tell them to ask a neighbor, but this causes talking and disruption for the others. Frankly, it's also unfair to the neighbor.

Any ideas for me?

Carolyn in New Hampshire

Dear Carolyn,

Experienced teachers have a distinct strategy when they give directions. Here are the steps to follow:

1. Wait until you have the attention of the entire class.
2. Pause dramatically and state the directions clearly, one time only.
3. Then check for understanding by having a student repeat the directions.
4. Write the directions on the board, including page number and all other important details.

If someone says, "I don't get it," point to the board. Do not repeat directions. Stating directions one time, clearly and simply, is the best way to have students focus. If they know you'll repeat things, they won't feel the need to listen the first time.

When you are clear and firm, everyone benefits!

"Yeah!" respond at least a few of the children. Hands go up immediately with suggestions while other children shout out ideas.

Maintain control. "I think we'll play a game. Which short games are your favorites? And please, people, no shouting out ideas. Raise your hands."

"I think we should play Higher/Lower," says a girl with curly hair.

Another hand goes up, and you nod to acknowledge a freckle-faced boy. "I think we should play the Unique Game."

"Okay," you say, "let's play the Unique Game, and don't worry, next time we'll play Higher/Lower."

Once the choice is made, have the student who suggested the game explain the rules to you and the class.

What are the *observable* characteristics of a good teacher?

I currently work at Florida Atlantic University where I supervise student teachers. My job is to observe student teachers as they present lessons in a real classroom and provide them with constructive feedback.

I can recall the very first observation I ever conducted. The teacher was a young woman, Pilar Mendez, who had a slight accent. In the first few moments of observation, I became concerned that her accent might hurt her ability to communicate, but as I observed her, I realized that my initial concern was groundless.

Pilar had what I call "the gift." She was a natural teacher— excellent instincts, a calm and loving style, and subtle, yet effective, classroom control.

As I observed, Pilar presented a math lesson on the fact family for the numbers 6, 7, and 13. She drew a house on the board and wrote the related numbers in the attic of the house.

"Class, I am going to tell you a story about a very special family," she said. "The numbers 6, 7, and 13 are all members of this special family, and they all live in the attic of this house. They want to go into the rooms on the first and second floors, but they want to be in each room together."

Pilar then represented the facts for each "room."

"Now you are going to make your own house with different fact families. You will make number sentences, too. Be sure not to leave out any member of the family when writing the number sentences," she warned the students.

Pilar used the family metaphor beautifully and made the math lesson real for the students. She told an engaging story for each fact family. She brought the lesson alive and turned a potentially dry lesson into something the children enjoyed.

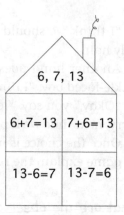

6, 7, 13

6+7=13   7+6=13

13-6=7   13-7=6

The students were attentive and involved. When she asked questions to check for understanding, she praised them with gusto, always using their names and thanking them for listening. In short, she had the students eating out of her hand.

Now that I have been observing student teachers for many years, I have noticed some interesting patterns. I can tell whether a teacher will be successful in the first five minutes of the lesson. There are certain qualities that good teachers possess, and I feel that many of us are born with those qualities. If you are lucky, you are one of those people. If not, you can learn to be effective by watching good teachers and practicing good teaching skills.

What qualities do I need to be effective in the classroom?

To be honest, "the gift" cannot be learned. You have it, or you don't. You should try to observe excellent teachers and look for the following characteristics. You can be a wonderful teacher if you try hard to develop these qualities:

- You must be confident. Even if you're not . . . you have to fake it!
- You must present yourself as a person who is in *control*.
- You must present a kind and caring aura.
- Your voice must have inflection, vary your volume for effect. (See the Voice chapter.)

- You must have good "people skills." A good sub is able to assess the emotional needs of each student and then act to meet those needs.
- You must be organized. Arrive early so that you can look through the material and understand your subject matter.
- You must be flexible, reacting to unexpected situations without becoming flustered.
- You must always maintain your sense of humor.

Remember that part of teaching is *acting*! It may be that in your personal life you don't exude confidence, your normal speaking voice is monotone, and your bedroom closet is somewhat disorganized. When you teach, however, you have to act the part, and that means you must project a confident demeanor, a singsong voice, and an organized approach. If you do enough acting, you may actually acquire these traits in everything you do.

Summary

If you want to be a better substitute teacher, recognize the power of observation—look, listen, and learn. As a sub, you are in a unique position to observe good teachers and other experienced subs. The following guidelines will help you as you observe:

- Observe the layout and organization of every classroom you enter. Use a notebook to record good ideas.
- Try to visually observe a good teacher or an experienced sub. Note the techniques that are used to present content, manage the class, and interact with students.
- Don't be afraid to ask questions. (See the Mentors chapter.)
- Observe your students. They can teach you much about the classroom, and more important, they provide instant feedback about techniques that work and those that don't.

- Learn how to develop the qualities that every effective teacher has. You may not have the natural gift for teaching, but you can develop the skills that are needed.

A good substitute teacher keeps his or her eyes and ears open. You're a teacher, but to get better, you must be an observer, too.

Positive Expectations

As Barbara Laster walked toward her assigned classroom at Pumpkin Patch School, she marveled at how quiet the halls could be at 7:30 in the morning. A new sub with only five assignments to her credit, Barbara was doing well. Sure, there were times when things got a little sketchy, but overall, she was pleased with her own progress. *Just remember*, she thought as she walked, *look for really good teachers and try to emulate them.*

When she reached her second-grade classroom, she noticed that her grade partner was already in the adjoining room. Barbara went next door to introduce herself.

"Hi," she said with a smile. "I'm Barbara Laster, and I'll be subbing for Mrs. Goldman today."

The other teacher looked up and smiled warmly. She was a petite blond in her early forties.

"Hi, Barbara. I'm Kelly Webster. If you need anything or have any questions, please feel free."

Barbara and Kelly talked for a few moments. As she walked back to her classroom, Barbara sensed that Kelly Webster was one of those "good teachers."

Throughout the day, Barbara noticed that older students would wander into Kelly's class and give her a hug. It appeared that every child in the school loved her. *I hope that'll be me someday*, Barbara thought.

The second-grade students went to PE late in the day, and Barbara and Kelly had a few minutes to talk. Just as they started, a tall, young man, wearing a University of Connecticut T-shirt, knocked on the door frame.

"Jonathan!" Kelly exclaimed. "It's wonderful to see you! How's college?"

They hugged and both seemed to get teary-eyed. Barbara said she had a few things to do in her classroom and left them to their reunion.

After the students were dismissed for the day, Barbara wandered back to Kelly's classroom.

"That seemed like a nice reunion . . . with that young man," Barbara said.

"Oh, you mean Jonathan? Yes," Kelly paused as if thinking of something in the past. "That's quite a story."

"Tell me," said Barbara with a smile.

"Jonathan was my student during my very first year of teaching. His parents were worried that he might have severe learning problems, and, frankly, so was I. He was messy, with poor coordination, and he never finished his work. His seatwork was atrocious. Each day I would write on his papers things like *Jonathan, please try harder*, or *Jonathan, this is so messy that I can't read it*, or *Sloppy work*. But, things only got worse."

Barbara frowned. "What did you do?"

"Well, one day, I decided to try something new. Even though his work was just as sloppy as it always was, I wrote *Jonathan, much better!*"

Barbara looked puzzled. "But, Kelly, it wasn't any better. You said so yourself."

"That's true," said Kelly, "but I figured that a positive approach couldn't hurt. Negative comments certainly weren't working."

"So you kept writing positive things about awful work?" asked Barbara.

"Yep. For three weeks Jonathan's work continued to be awful! But I wrote positive notes each day," Kelly shrugged. "No change. So with every passing day I made my comments more glowing."

Barbara laughed. "What happened?"

"One day I noticed a slight improvement. It wasn't much, but it was noticeable. I continued to praise his work."

"Did the improvement continue?"

"It did. And by the end of the school year, Jonathan had fine penmanship and was doing really good work! It was pretty amazing."

"All because you said good things to him? *That's* pretty amazing."

Kelly smiled. "He had it in him. We just needed to find a way to get it out. When he came in today, he told me that he's majoring in business at UConn and that today he received notice that he had made the Dean's List! He said he felt he had to come and share the good news with me."

Now it was Barbara's turn to get teary-eyed.

Kelly had *positive expectations* for all of her students, and in Jonathan's case, her positive comments led to positive results. Obviously, a situation like Jonathan's is unusual, but things like that can and do happen in teaching. Kelly Webster proved it!

In their classic text *The First Days of School*, Harry and Rosemary Wong identify three characteristics that all good teachers exhibit. In the book, they make the argument that every good teacher

1. has positive expectations for student success
2. is a good classroom manager
3. knows how to design lessons for student mastery

If you want to be a good substitute teacher, it's important for you to have these characteristics. In this chapter, we'll focus our attention on the first, *positive expectations*.

Why is it so important to have positive expectations?

Children have a remarkable ability to "read" a teacher's attitude. They can size you up instantly. Your tone of voice, your body language, the way you walk, and the way you look all contribute to your image. If the image you project is positive, your students will pick up on your confidence, warmth, and acceptance and respond in kind.

Positive expectations establish a positive classroom culture. You expect the students to do their very best. You are so sure of your positive opinion of the class that there is no question that the students will perform well for you. And because the students know that they'll be rewarded for good work (even if the rewards are only a smile and a kind word), they'll try hard to earn your praise.

How can you show students that you have positive expectations for them?

There are specific things you can say and do that lead to a positive expectations culture. Two vignettes might help illustrate.

- A colleague, Jan McCoy, once told me that on the first day of school she always told her fifth-grade class, "Right now, you all have an A in every subject! All you have to do is to keep it that way, and I think I can!"
- Another colleague, Carlos Aguilar, took a long-term subbing assignment for a middle school math teacher. One of his students, Andrea, came up to his desk one day during study hall.

  "Mr. Aguilar, I've always hated math, and geometry was impossible for me. But since you took over our class, I'm sort of getting it. A little, at least."

Carlos smiled. "Well, you're a very smart girl, Andrea. I think you're going to do very well in geometry. In fact, I know you are!"

In the first vignette, Jan McCoy could have said the usual things, "you'll have to work hard to get an A." Or worse, "only the very best students get A's in my class." But she didn't. Instead she let every student know that they were A material (even if they weren't) and implied, without ever saying it, that an A grade was theirs to lose and that hard work would allow them to keep it.

In the second vignette, Carlos Aguilar used positive expectations in a very effective way. But before he could do that, he had to project a positive attitude that convinced Andrea he liked her. He was always helpful, never critical. As a consequence, and in order to please a teacher she liked, Andrea studied her geometry each night. Carlos called on her often, and Andrea liked the response when she gave the right answer! The praise that she received built up her confidence.

Earlier I mentioned that one of the most gratifying aspects of being a substitute teacher is that you can give each student a "fresh start." This is particularly true for those students who feel no connection with the classroom teacher. By using positive expectations, you can let these students believe that you are genuinely interested in them. They will eagerly rise to the occasion.

How can you be positive when the students are negative?

Although there are no easy answers to this question, there are strategies you can use when you encounter a negative class. There will always be a few students who deserve your positive response. Initially, focus on them, giving praise and voicing approval. At least some of the negative students may modify their attitudes quickly so that they can get some of your "positive vibes." Then broaden your focus to include these students.

And the students who just won't come around? Manage them, but expend your energy on those who want to learn.

Thank the students who are listening. Reward good behavior whenever possible, and ignore negativity. After some time passes, negative students will recognize that they cannot get your attention or upset you with poor performance or behavior. In many cases, the negative behavior will cease.

A confident substitute teacher praises often and points out negative behavior rarely. If you find yourself correcting students more than you are praising them, you should rebalance the scales in favor of praise.

What is the best way to praise student conduct?

Whenever you praise a student, try to praise in an *authentic* way. This implies that you do more than say "good job" or "nice work." Authentic praise is warm and caring. It comes from the heart, engages the students, and encourages them to want to answer questions, behave well, and work cooperatively.

When you want to praise an individual student, you should try to use specific praise. For example, let's assume that you're teaching social studies and you ask for the definition of a *peninsula*.

A student, Ryan, raises his hand and responds with, "A peninsula is a piece of land that projects into water but is connected to the mainland."

You nod, smile in approval, and say, "Thank you, Ryan, you're right! A peninsula is a piece of land that projects into the water but is connected to the mainland. You must have been studying last night!"

You've used specific praise by using Ryan's name and repeating his answer for reinforcement. You added a personal comment ("studying last night") to add warmth and make the praise authentic as well as specific. You sounded interested in Ryan's answer and appreciative of his intelligence. But you've also done something else. You've encouraged other students to

What should I do when a student says, "That's not fair"?

Dear Barbara,

I find that when I sub, the students are very focused on the concept of fairness. Certain children feel as if they are being singled out or picked on for their misbehavior, and they invariably respond with the dreaded comment "That's not fair."

I try to be fair at all times, but there are situations when I must enforce rules. It doesn't seem to matter whether I focus on the entire class or single out certain individuals, I still hear that it's not fair.

Is there any way to be sure that I am fair at all times?

Dan in Massachusetts

Dear Dan,

The simple answer to your question is no.

All teachers hear the "not fair" comment. No student believes that she deserves a consequence for disruptive or inappropriate behavior. From the student's point of view, she did nothing wrong. Hence, any reaction by you is "unfair."

When children say "it's not fair," they are attempting to manipulate you. Because it's your job to manage the classroom, you must stand firm and maintain order. Try to manage the classroom with fairness, but when the need arises, state consequences with authority—without guilt or unease. If it's not 100 percent fair, so be it. It is the student's responsibility to behave, and if she doesn't, it was her actions, not yours, that have caused the consequence.

One way to ensure fairness is to uncover the true cause of the disruption. Never punish the whole group for the actions of just one child. Isolate the offender, give him a warning, and then follow through with your consequence. If you see two or three students seriously misbehaving, act quickly with a warning and then give them a referral on the spot. This will set a tone for the others.

participate, knowing that they might get a positive response like Ryan did.

This same technique works for student conduct. When you see someone behaving in a positive manner, walk over to him and thank him, using his name. State what you have seen.

For example, "Leshaun, I see you had your book out and were ready for the lesson to begin. I appreciate that, and I will be sure to leave that information in my note to your teacher today."

Why is it important to be positive with your colleagues?

People enjoy working with professionals who have a positive outlook on their job and on life in general. People tend to avoid someone who is always negative. So even if you're having a bad day, keep a smile on your face and project a positive image. Staying positive has no downside. Why not be an upbeat, positive person?

Every school is like a large family that is protective and sensitive to criticism. You would be wise to keep critical comments to yourself. It's in poor taste to bite the hand that feeds you. If you complain about your classroom assignment, the course content, your students, or other teachers, you may have guaranteed that you will not get another invitation to teach at that school.

In the Ethics chapter, I noted that some teachers love to complain and gossip about administrators, colleagues, parents, and students. Listen politely, but don't engage in this kind of negative (and unprofessional as well as ethically dubious) behavior.

Being positive, whether it is with students or colleagues, is a state of mind. Look for things to praise, no matter how small. Be a good listener. Be understanding. Never be judgmental about a colleague or a parent. If you do those things, you will have achieved the key characteristic that is exhibited by all good teachers.

Summary

If you expect good things from your students and encourage them with praise at every opportunity, good things will happen in a classroom. To establish an atmosphere in which positive expectations work to your advantage, follow these guidelines:

- Project a positive attitude every time you walk into a classroom. Students have a remarkable ability to read your tone of voice, your body language, the way you walk, your entire persona. Be sure that you project confidence, warmth, and acceptance.
- Be helpful and positive, never critical. Before students perform for you, they have to feel some personal connection. If you create a warm, nurturing atmosphere in which good work gets high praise and even average work (but with sincere effort) gets a positive comment, you establish a classroom culture that will lead to academic excellence.
- When most students are negative, focus your attention and praise on those few who are positive. Over time, broaden your attention and praise to others who are trying. Always remain positive.
- Use authentic and specific praise. Whenever you praise the class or an individual student, make sure you mean it. Be warm and encouraging. When you praise an individual, use her name, indicate why her work is praiseworthy, and add a personal touch.
- Be positive in your dealings with other teachers and administrators. Even if you're having a bad day, keep a smile on your face and project a positive image. It can only work to your benefit.

Students respond best when they encounter a teacher who has positive expectations. You can be one of those teachers. You know—a teacher that students remember years afterward. Be positive!

Questioning Techniques

"**W**ho can identify and tell me about the main character in the story we just read?" asked Samantha Smith, a substitute teacher in the fourth grade at Woodland Hills Elementary.

As she slowly walked around the classroom, five hands shot up into the air. Samantha smiled at the enthusiastic response but waited for even more hands to rise. After she was satisfied with the level of participation, she paused dramatically and then chose someone to answer.

"Jared?"

"I think the main character was Jackie Robinson. He was really a hero."

"Good answer, Jared. But why did you choose Jackie Robinson over Branch Rickey?"

"Well, even though Mr. Rickey was the manager of the Dodgers at that time, Jackie Robinson was the brave one, in my opinion."

"Why was Mr. Robinson more of a hero than Mr. Rickey?"

Three other hands went up accompanied by a few "oohs" and "aahs."

"I can see we have a few more opinions. I'm pleased," Samantha said with a big smile. "Jared, may I get some other opinions?"

"Sure, Ms. Smith."

"Madison, tell me who you think was the hero of our story and please explain why."

As the discussion moved forward, Samantha Smith was able to elevate the discussion by using effective questioning techniques. The students were comparing and contrasting character traits. They were analyzing levels of courage and suggesting modern equivalents from people in today's news.

When the bell rang, the class groaned collectively. They were enjoying themselves and wanted the discussion to continue. Samantha Smith knew that she had done a fine job. *That's what good teaching is all about*, she thought.

Good teachers never lecture. They prefer to make their point by asking questions and encouraging discussion. They look for that "a-ha" moment of self-discovery. When students acquire knowledge from their peers, their retention and appreciation of the information improves. Learning via discussion is much more effective than hearing it from a podium.

As a substitute teacher, one of the ways that you can earn respect and maintain control is to run an interesting class. From the students' perspective, *interesting* means that things happen that involve them—actively, repeatedly, and enjoyably. Students always prefer to speak themselves and to listen to their classmates rather than listen to you! Lecturing is a sure way to lose the group.

A skilled teacher can gently guide a discussion to make a point or impart important learning. To accomplish this, you must learn how to ask effective questions.

What are the keys to good questioning techniques?

In order to ask a good question, you must have a firm grasp of the material under discussion and appreciate its meaning and context. Your questions should focus first on "obvious" information—those things that the majority of students will grasp. This includes factual information. In education we call these *low-order questions*. Once you get the entire class involved, you can move on to consider more creative and analytical information and relationships, *high-order questions*. As you begin asking questions and soliciting responses and discussion, follow these guidelines:

- **Don't rush!** After you've asked a question and the first hands go up, wait a few moments. Many students need time to understand and process the question and then formulate a response.
- **Use a proven questioning strategy.** The basic strategy is threefold. Ask a question (posed to the whole group), pause to allow children to think, and then call on one student to answer. Be sure that you have given all students enough time to understand and then formulate their responses. Many teachers count to five silently and slowly before choosing a student to answer.
- **Never say a child's name and then ask a question.** Studies have shown that other students will tune out if they know that they will not have to answer. Ask the whole group, and then choose your *responder*.
- **Always use positive and specific reinforcement when responding to an answer.** Try to use the student's name in your response. For example, say, "Thank you, Jared. That was very insightful. I'm glad you remembered some of Jackie Robinson's heroic acts." This type of response is pleasing to Jared and reinforces his answer for the rest of

the class. In addition, it encourages others to answer in hopes of obtaining some of your positive stroking.

If you take the time to get your students involved, they will respond. Your job is to draw them out, and a solid questioning strategy will help you do that.

Are there different kinds of questions?

Yes, there are different kinds of questions, and good teachers ask them in a specific order. These teachers begin with questions about basic factual knowledge and build up to questions that invoke higher level thinking. If we again consider the Jackie Robinson story, an initial question might be: "Who can tell me when Jackie Robinson played baseball?" or "Who can tell me the city and team Jackie Robinson played for?" In asking these questions you stress basic factual knowledge and, as a consequence, involve all students who read the story.

As the questions and responses continue, a transition to high-order questions allows your students to consider the subtleties of the story. A high-order question like "There are a number of important characters in this story. Who do you think was the real hero?" forces students to consider many facts about the characters and their relationships to one another and the story as a whole. The question allows students to be analytical and to form opinions about the information they have learned.

You can create a discussion that raises awareness and promotes understanding by structuring the order of your questions. When you want to reach those high-order questions, be sure to use words and phrases such as *why, how, explain the differences, organize those thoughts and describe, can you predict,* and *can you compare.*

A useful way to organize your questions is to follow Bloom's taxonomy.[1] Bloom's taxonomy of educational objectives, devel-

---

1. An excellent discussion of Bloom's taxonomy can be found at learningand teaching.info/learning/bloomtax.htm.

oped in the 1950s but still relevant today, lists six levels of cognitive operations: knowledge, comprehension, application, analysis, synthesis, and evaluation. Questions that focus on knowledge check basic facts about people, places, and things. Comprehension questions check for the student's broader understanding of a topic. Application questions encourage students to use knowledge for problem solving. Analysis questions help students explore the smaller elements of a larger topic. Synthesis prods students to use basic knowledge in a creative way, and evaluation questions encourage judgments and predictions.

Tom Drummond[2] provides us with an excellent example of a good classroom dialogue, reaching higher levels of questioning.

- **Description:** *What did you see? What happened? What is the difference between . . . ?*
- **Common Purpose:** *What is the purpose or function of . . . ?*
- **Procedures:** *How was this done? What will have to be done?*
- **Possibilities:** *What else could . . . ? How could we . . . ?*
- **Prediction:** *What will happen next?*
- **Justification:** *How can you tell? What evidence led you to . . . ?*
- **Rationale for reality:** *Why? What is the reason?*
- **Generalization:** *What is the same about . . . and . . . ? What could you generalize from these events?*
- **Definition:** *What does . . . mean?*

When you plan a lesson that will involve lots of Q&A, you might consider selecting questions from a number of these categories. Doing so will keep the questions interesting and force your students to look at many different facets of the subject matter.

---

2. Drummond, Tom. "A Brief Summary of the Best Practices in Teaching." Available at http://northonline.sccd.ctc.edu/eceprog/bstprac.htm.

How should I prepare for a special needs class?

Dear Barbara,

I have been asked to sub in a special needs classroom next week and I'm a bit uneasy. I have had very little experience with special education classrooms. Will the children have emotional problems, learning disabilities, physical problems, autism? Will there be an aide to help me? I don't know what to expect.

Please advise me on the best way to prepare for this kind of situation.

Rosa in Dallas

Dear Rosa,

You should not be concerned about subbing in a classroom for special needs children. Because the setting and level of needs varies tremendously, try to get as much information as you can in advance. If possible, stop by and meet, call, or e-mail the teacher. The more you know ahead of time, the better.

You'll encounter many different variations when you are asked to sub in a special needs setting. You might work in a Resource Room. Students flow in and out, and you will work with small groups. Students may bring work from their classes, and you will help them complete their assignments. This scenario is called a "pull-out program."

You may be asked to go from room to room and assist children in their regular classroom setting. In this case, you will get your guidance from the classroom teacher.

The most challenging setting is the self-contained special education classroom. You will probably have a small group for the whole day. Law requires that the teacher-student ratio be small, so there will always be a supportive paraprofessional working with you. The paraprofessional will know the classroom routine. If you want to have a successful day, be sure to follow it. Never be afraid to ask for help from the administration if things get away from you. Trust your instincts and get help when necessary.

Try to get to know your students. Be supportive and positive. They, like all children, thrive on your praise. If you treat them with respect, the rewards will be great!

Should I encourage students to ask questions?

Many subs shy away from encouraging student questions, particularly when the subject matter (e.g., science) is not their area of expertise. Stated bluntly, the sub doesn't want to look stupid. I think this is a mistake and short-circuits an important opportunity for learning.

Encourage your students to ask questions. Even if you're unsure of the answer, another student might have it if you open the question to classroom discussion. And if no one knows, don't hesitate to admit that you're unsure (a little self-deprecating humor might help). But don't stop there! Promise the students that you'll find out and tell them later in the day. During a break, refer to the Teacher's Guide for the textbook you're using—it often has the answer you're looking for. And if that doesn't work, have a student look up the information on the Web.

What is the "correct pause time," and why is it so important?

You'll recall that our first guideline for asking effective questions is *don't rush*. But proper pacing for one teacher might be radically different from proper pacing for another. And that's okay—your style and personality will dictate the rhythm of your questions. But it's also important to note that if your pause time is too short, you'll inadvertently exclude many children from the discussion. And if it's too long, you may risk boring some of the better students.

As I noted, the general guideline for pause time after posing a question is about five seconds before choosing a student to respond. This brief silence helps students think about what was asked and lets them reflect on the right response. As important, the silence increases the dramatic effect of the question and serves to further engage the students. It takes a confident teacher to feel comfortable with the silence, and as a sub, you need to foster that feeling of confidence. Any time you have silence in a classroom, you know you are on the right track.

Is there a correct way to ask a question?

A good question elicits information and at the same time enhances learning. The following guidelines will help you ask good questions:

- **Try to state your questions clearly, using a single statement.** The longer the question, the more difficult it will be to understand and answer.
- **Avoid repeating a question.** If you repeat your questions regularly, students will feel as if they do not need to listen the first time.
- **Be sure that you make eye contact with as many students as possible when asking a question.** Your intent is to draw as many students as possible into the discussion, and making eye contact personalizes your approach.
- **Call on a variety of students.** It's natural to call on the student whose hand is up and who you are sure knows the correct answer. Try to draw out the quiet ones. It's also natural to call on the student who misbehaves, just to keep him or her in the discussion. This is fine, but don't forget the others.

Summary

A good teacher imparts information by asking questions and encouraging discussion. If you learn to ask questions effectively, your students will become more actively involved in each lesson. The following guidelines will help:

- **Ask both low- and high-order questions.** Your intent should be to draw students in with relatively straightforward factual questions and then move into questions that require more thought and analysis.

- **Don't rush.** Try to pause five seconds before accepting an answer.
- **Use a proven questioning strategy.** Ask a question, pause to allow children to think, and then call on one student to answer.
- **Use positive reinforcement.** Be sure to respond to answers using specific praise and reinforce (restate) the correct answer.
- **Ask different kinds of questions.** Have the students describe, justify, predict, and generalize as part of your questioning technique.
- **Encourage students to ask you questions.** This creates a dialogue that can only improve the classroom atmosphere.
- **Follow guidelines for asking "good" questions.** Use the guidelines in this book or refer to many other guidelines available on the Web.

The art and science of asking good questions is a skill that you'll hone as you gain classroom experience. If you master the skill, you will improve your students' learning significantly.

Relationships

My day as a sub in a fourth-grade classroom seemed typical. I took attendance without incident and was about to begin the morning activities when a short, brown-haired boy with freckles across the bridge of his nose approached me.

"Uh, Mrs. Pressman," he said, staring at his shoes and then sneaking an eager look at my face. "Would it, uh, be okay if I take the attendance folder to the office?"

I smiled and nodded. "Sure, and thanks for the help! What's your name?"

"Jason," he said with a shy smile. He met my eyes for the first time.

All through the day, Jason seemed to stay by my side. He asked to help hand out materials, and when there was a lull, he told me stories about himself. I noticed that he spent more time with me than with his classmates.

As the day continued, I sensed that Jason was not well liked. I couldn't understand why because he seemed to be a nice boy. But during recess, I noticed that other children excluded him from their games. After a few minutes, Jason wandered over to me, and again we talked until the bell rang. He was a sweet boy, and I actually enjoyed our conversation.

That evening, my husband and I attended a concert at the local high school. During intermission, three people approached me. I recognized Jason and waved. I assumed that the adults were his parents. As they approached, I introduced myself and told them what a lovely son they had.

Jason's mom, almost in tears, thanked me for being so kind to her son. She said that Jason told her that I was the nicest teacher he had ever had. She whispered that he was having a tough year socially, and today had been a rare wonderful day for him. Jason and his parents left to return to their seats, but only after the mother gave me a gentle hug.

Taking the time to establish a relationship with a child has its own special rewards. Making a difference in a child's life, even if it's only for a single day, matters.

Sadly, there are some substitute teachers who feel that building relationships with their students just isn't worth the effort. "After all," they argue, "I'm there for just one day and then I leave. My job is to keep the class under control and present the teaching materials. That's it."

I disagree! As a sub, you have the unique opportunity to foster meaningful relationships with children. Because you're not there each day, every child in the class has an opportunity for a fresh start with you. Kind words of encouragement and a warm smile can do wonders for a child who may not get enough attention from the regular classroom teacher.

Relationships *do* matter, and they're always worth the effort. In this chapter, we'll discuss relationships with your students, your teaching colleagues, and other members of the school community.

Is it possible to build a relationship in a single day?

I'm sure you've heard the phrase *random acts of kindness*. Someone you don't know and will likely never see again does something to help you or encourage you or support you in a time of need. You may not remember the person's name or even what he or she looked like, but you will remember the act of kindness, possibly for your entire life.

In a way, a single act of kindness establishes a bond—a relationship—between two people. When you interact with the children in your classrooms, remember that an act of kindness establishes a bond with each of them. The teacher-student interaction may take less than a minute, but a relationship has been established. Build on it.

There's something else you should remember about relationships with students. If you take the time to establish, cultivate, and build on them, there's a direct pragmatic benefit for you. Building these bonds will serve you well for the next time that you will be subbing in a particular school. Students talk about subs, and if you have a good reputation with the students, you will command greater respect. The bottom line: establishing and cultivating student relationships will make your job easier. And that's always a good thing.

So, how do I build a relationship?

The answer is complicated and simple at the same time. You have to sense what a child needs and then try hard to give it to him or her. Above all, you have to be an observer first, listening and watching each child. Observe their demeanor, their interaction with others, their classroom presence.

Building relationships is all about kindness and respect, reassurance and discipline, but most important, it's about doing what needs to be done to help a child. Recently, I ran an orientation session for student teachers at Florida Atlantic University. The intent of the session was to begin preparation for their student teaching experience, then two weeks away. One of the many topics of discussion we covered was this one:

"How do you handle the child who has a proverbial 'kick me' sign on his back?"

I explained that every class seems to have one child who is an outsider, who other children ostracize or pick on. It's more common than most people might think. I asked my group of new student teachers how they would handle the situation.

There was a long pause, and then a young education major raised her hand tentatively.

"I *was* that child," she said. "In fourth grade my parents were going through a divorce, and I acted out against my classmates, my teachers, just about everybody. The kids in my class reciprocated. No one would play with me. Kids made fun of me. It was awful."

I thought she was just reinforcing my comment about "kick me" children, but then she continued. "One day my teacher asked if I wanted to have lunch, just the two of us."

I could see that the young woman was getting emotional just recalling the incident, but I said nothing.

"We, you know, talked about things, and my teacher asked if we could do it again in a few days, and we did. A few days later she asked another student to join the two of us. We talked and even laughed. For the first time that school year, I felt really special."

She swallowed hard, and I could see tears in her eyes. "A few days later she asked two more kids to join the group at lunch. Before long those kids were talking to me all the time."

"To tell the truth," she said in a shaky voice, "it was that moment that I decided to become a teacher."

Take the time to build relationships with your students. Fourteen years from now, someone might relate a wonderful story about you.

Is it worth taking the time to build relationships with the full-time staff?

Be prepared for one harsh reality. When you walk in the front door of the school as a substitute teacher, you won't always

How should I proceed when I'm warned about a problem student?

Dear Barbara,

I was subbing in a third-grade classroom when the principal stopped in and asked if I'd be able to sub next week in the sixth grade. Of course, I said yes. At the end of the day, I stopped in to see the sixth-grade classroom teacher to introduce myself and get pertinent information about the class.

The classroom teacher warned me that Christopher (not his real name) could be a real problem, and I should beware.

Now I'm concerned. I don't want to get off on the wrong foot with Christopher. I don't want to single him out.

What should I do with the information I was given?

Mike in Los Angeles

Dear Mike,

You are very fortunate to have the information about Christopher in advance. If possible, try to learn even more about him before you begin class. Are his problems emotional? Does he have learning disabilities that contribute to his frustration? Does he like to show off to cover up for limitations?

Armed with information, you can decide how to approach Christopher. You should be proactive. Make a connection with him early in the day, such as "Christopher is a special name for me, my favorite nephew is Christopher. He even looks a little like you." Ask him where the teacher keeps the attendance folder. Ask him to run an errand for you. Compliment him on his cool haircut.

These techniques should help. However, be ready for a confrontation. No matter how well you handle this troubled child, something may set him off during the day and you will have to deal with his behavior. If you must, make use of the classroom management plan, warnings, referrals, and detentions. Don't be afraid to get serious. But with a little TLC, you and Christopher will have a good day together.

be recognized as a legitimate member of the faculty. But you can earn that status by being friendly and interested in your colleagues. Say good morning to them. Ask about their classes and their families. Tell them about the last time you subbed in their classrooms. Ask how a difficult student is doing. By showing interest, you will slowly gain their respect.

Don't feel hurt if you are not included in conversation in the teachers' lounge. This is a place where private conversation is important. Just smile and listen. The longer you work in one school, the more involved you will become in casual conversation.

As I mentioned earlier, I *never* participate in school gossip. It's highly unprofessional and can sometimes cause problems for you in the long run. Keep your standards high, and the faculty will respect you. If an opportunity for a long-term position comes along, the principal may ask faculty members what they know about you. If the responses include phrases like "competent teacher," "very professional," "really friendly," and "gets along well with everybody," it's likely the position will be yours.

How should I interact with other school personnel?

The secretary (a.k.a. administrative assistant) in the front office is probably one of the most powerful people in the school. She has the ear of the principal at all times. She also has the ear of students, teachers, parents, and administrators. She hears all the gossip. She knows where the keys are and where supplies can be found.

Learn her name. Always say good morning and good-bye. Make pleasant small talk with her. She deserves your respect and interest. She has a hard job, and if she becomes your ally, your life in that school will be much, much easier.

In some classrooms, you'll work with paraprofessionals (e.g., teacher's aides), who can be very helpful. Although they'll be familiar with the classroom routine and every child's name and quirks, you shouldn't feel intimidated by the paraprofessional. Use his or her knowledge and always express your thanks for the help, but remember that you're the teacher. Be a strong and confident team leader.

What about interacting with nonteaching staff?

If you've been granted a long-term subbing assignment at a school, it's time to make friends with the custodial staff. A kind word and smile, coupled with respect for the hard work they do, will do wonders when something needs to be fixed.

During one long-term assignment, I built a friendly relationship with the school custodian, Frank. I noticed that whenever Frank came into the classroom, Jared, a young boy with severe learning disabilities, would be fascinated by his tool belt, the work he did, his blue work shirt, everything!

Somehow Frank sensed this and always asked the boy if he'd like to help. With a huge smile, Jared would nod until I thought his head would fall off. Before long, Jared was Frank's "assistant." This wonderful man, who got a GED late in life, took Jared under his wing and became an in-school father figure for the boy. One day, Jared came to me and asked whether Frank could read a story for the whole class. The custodian became the teacher. It's an experience that I'll never forget.

Needless to say, whenever I needed an extra desk or a new pencil sharpener, those items appeared instantly!

Summary

When you foster special relationships, they pay both short-term and long-term benefits. Although it takes a little extra effort, it's easy if you follow the advice in this chapter.

- Building relationships with students, faculty, and other staff will pay dividends when you return to the school for your next assignment. You're a known quantity, respected and recognized as a "real teacher." Your life will be easier.
- Try to sense what a child needs, and then try hard to give it to him or her. Observe and listen to each of the children.

Observe their demeanor, their interaction with others, their classroom presence.
- Cultivate a friendly interaction with at least some members of the full-time faculty. If they come to know you and respect you, their good words may help you land a long-term subbing assignment or even a full-time position.
- Make the school secretary your ally. She knows everything and can help you learn the ropes.
- Become a friend with the school custodian if you're in a long-term assignment. When things need to be fixed, it's nice to have the custodian on your side.

Good teachers love to interact with people. Use that gift to build solid relationships throughout the school.

Survival Techniques

Jan Sommerville walked into her assigned classroom at J. P. Evans Middle School and sensed that it would be a hard day. The classroom had a bad vibe—noisy, chaotic—she couldn't quite put her finger on it, but it was there nonetheless.

As she got to her desk, she noticed one very tall young man, obviously a class leader, talking boisterously in the back of the room. He glanced in her direction with a look of disdain and went right back to his loud conversation.

"Good morning. My name is Mrs. Sommerville," Jan said, far too tentatively. The class paid little attention.

Jan paused a moment. "Okay, let's settle down," she said a bit more forcefully. A few students turned in her direction and stopped talking, but the group in the back, led by the tall boy, paid no attention.

Jan tried again, but there was still conversation going on. A girl in the front row raised her hand, "Um, Mrs. Sommers, it's 8:45 and we have to line up for PE."

Jan nodded.

"It's Mrs. *Sommerville*. Thanks for telling me, but this class goes nowhere," she said assertively, "until we quiet down so that I can get the morning attendance and lunch count ready for the office."

"That's not fair," said the tall boy. "We've got gym, and it's the best class of the day." His friends laughed and seconded his comments.

Jan smiled. "Life's not fair . . . what's your name?"

"Darrell," the tall boy said roughly.

"Life's not always fair, Darrell," she said. "But I can be fair today if you follow my classroom rules. And my rules say you stay right here until we get our morning work done."

She paused for effect. "So, you can talk or you can let me take attendance and then you can go to PE."

Jan immediately picked those students who were quiet, asked their names, checked them off the attendance list, and had them line up for PE. Students learned that going to PE was something that they would have to earn.

The last person in the line was Darrell, who had continued to be boisterous throughout. As the class filed out of the room, Jan stepped in front of Darrell.

"I'd like you to stay for a minute," she said emphatically, looking steadily into his eyes.

Darrell became very quiet. They talked briefly, but Jan sensed that she shouldn't push too hard. She simply thanked Darrell for his cooperation now, and then walked with him to PE, checking to be sure that the others arrived on time. She explained Darrell's situation to Coach Scott, who also had a talk with Darrell.

As an experienced sub, Jan Somerville had been through situations like this before. She knew that to maintain order she would have to hold something back. Her *survival technique* in this case was to hold back a privilege.

Luckily, the timing of the PE class fit her situation perfectly. She was able to establish order and confront the student who represented her most serious behavior challenge. Her timing enabled her to speak with Darrell in private without giving him an opportunity to put on a show for his friends. Darrell might continue to be a challenge, but at least now he understood that Jan would not tolerate disruptive behavior and that she would confront him if he did disrupt. At some level he understood that there was really no point in making her life miserable.

There are some classes and some classroom situations that you simply want to survive. Every experienced teacher develops a set of survival techniques for use in such situations. In this chapter, we'll consider some of these techniques.

How strict should I be?

In an ideal world, all classroom and behavior management would be accomplished with kind words and positive reinforcement. But in the world of real classrooms and real students, it is sometimes necessary to set distinct behavior limits and reinforce them with strict measures when the limits are not followed.

The degree to which you must set firm or strict classroom rules varies from grade to grade and by the culture of each school. In general, middle school requires the most discipline and is the most likely setting for clear classroom policies. However, you cannot expect absolute silence in middle school. You'll need to be flexible. Classroom management is essential at the middle school level, but it must be handled with finesse and a sense of humor.

At every grade level, enter a new classroom with a positive attitude, giving the students every chance to exhibit acceptable behavior. But if "being nice" isn't working, quickly change your demeanor and become a no-nonsense classroom manager.

Are there any quick fixes?

If you enter a classroom that is out of control, recognize that it isn't your fault. The culture of the class and the mixture of students defines the manner in which students interact with one another and behave in general.

But those realities are cold comfort when you have to manage the class. Although there is no "silver bullet" that changes a challenging class into a good one, there are a number of quick fixes that you can use to modify unacceptable classroom behavior:

- **Hold back a privilege.** Learn what the students love to do and hold that activity hostage to good behavior. The students won't like it (and it is unfair to those students who are performing acceptably), but holding back a privilege can be an effective quick fix.
- **Isolate the instigator (there is always an instigator) and have a private conversation with him or her.** Tell the instigator that you do not want to embarrass him or her in front of other classmates, but the disruptive behavior will not be tolerated. Try to negotiate a path to better behavior. Often, this one-on-one talk in close proximity defuses the situation.
- **Promise a "fun activity" when work is done.** This approach works well in lower grades and often results in the children policing the behavior of others in order to ensure that the "fun activity" will be delivered.
- **Praise good behavior.** If a disruptive student does *anything* positive, praise him or her immediately and profusely. In some cases, this is all that will be required to modify behavior.
- **Let the students know that you'll tell the regular teacher who was good and who was not.** Put the names of both cooperative and uncooperative students on the board and promise to include each list in your teacher note. Provide some mechanism that enables a student on the uncooperative list to get his or her name removed.
- **Try to defuse a disruptive situation by refocusing the student on something interesting.** Use a brainteaser or some other filler to break up the situation. Promise to do it again later as a reward.

- **Don't be afraid to issue a detention slip or to send a student to the office.** If you do this, the rest of the class will see that you are serious about your standards of behavior. Others will be reluctant to push you if they see you follow through on standards of conduct.

When a class is difficult, your job is to manage it as best you can. As I've noted repeatedly, you must project confidence and control, even in a bad situation. If you look weak, you'll have trouble surviving the day.

How do I handle a real crisis?

When your best effort at applying a quick fix fails, you need to make some rapid decisions. You must assess whether or not the behavior can be tolerated for the rest of the day (or the remainder of the class period). If the behavior is tolerable, accept it and move on. As the day progresses and students become actively involved in their lessons, they may settle down. But if the classroom behavior is intolerable, you need to take action.

Here are some of your options:

- Seek the help of the teacher next door.
- Send the disruptive student or students to the office with a referral slip, calling ahead to alert the office.
- Send a note to the office with a trusted student that says you need the help of the principal.

It's important to emphasize that requesting help does not mean you've failed. It's far better to remove a disruptive student from the room than it is to allow that student to ruin everyone's day.

If I ask for help, will I be viewed as a weak teacher?

No, you will be viewed as someone who has self-respect and will not tolerate a disruptive or potentially dangerous situation. You are protecting yourself and the students when you

What should I do if a student reports suspicious behavior?

Dear Barbara,

I was subbing for the PE teacher today. We were outside on the field playing soccer. As we lined up to go inside, two girls came up to me and said that they saw a man taking pictures of them. I looked where they were pointing, but I didn't see anyone.

I wasn't sure whether this observation was real or imagined. I asked whether anyone else had seen this man. No one had. I decided to tell the principal about the incident, just in case. The principal thanked me and called the police to investigate. The whole school was "buzzing" about it. As it turns out, there was a man taking pictures, but he was surveying a piece of land for a development company! I felt embarrassed that I caused a "scene" for no reason.

Did I do the right thing by reporting the incident?

Brittany in Louisiana

Dear Brittany,

Congratulations! You handled the situation correctly. You really had no choice. If the girls were correct about a strange man taking pictures, there might have been a very serious threat. It's crucial for the police to be aware of it.

Regardless of whether the whole incident was real or imagined, you must take it seriously. You would be remiss to ignore a possible threat to your students. By notifying the administration, you allowed them to decide how to proceed. You acted in a very professional manner. Good job!

remove someone who will disrupt all learning and has the potential of putting the class in danger. Your responsibility as a teacher demands that you take action. The rest of the class will thank you silently.

The administration will recognize that you had the good judgment to take action before it was too late. And any other potentially disruptive students now understand that you mean business.

Are there any positive ways to restore order once it has been lost?

There is always hope! After you have subbed for a while, you will have a sense of which techniques will work for you. Try a few of the following tactics and see which ones work.

- It's a good idea to assess why your class is out of control. Is your material too difficult? Do students understand what to do? Perhaps you need to change the assignment or work on it as a group.
- If there is a personality conflict going on, remove the individuals and speak with them privately.
- Try standing near the misbehaving student or students. Use proximity to quiet the situation.
- Acknowledge the good things that are happening in the room and ignore the others. Rewarding good behavior can turn the mood of the class around.

Sometimes if you remain calm (never lose your composure) and just wait, the group will quiet down on its own. In the Difficult Day chapter, other classroom management ideas are discussed.

What if students ask to go to the restroom or to the nurse?

Allow *one child at a time* to leave your room, and be sure that student has a hall pass if the school requires one. Keep track of who is out of the room, the time that student left, and where he or she is going. Be sure the students understand that you will not be "gamed" into allowing them to roam the halls. If you see that there is a constant stream of students leaving for the bathroom, you must shut it down. Simply state that the bathroom trips are over for now.

Summary

Not every day in the classroom will be easy. In fact, some days will try your patience and, if you're not careful, crush your spirit. In order to avoid that, you have to develop a set of survival techniques for those days that are particularly challenging. The following guidelines will help:

- Be as strict as is required to control the class. You must set limits *and* enforce them.
- Try to isolate the cause of the classroom problem. Work to change things. If the subject matter is too difficult or unclear, for instance, do the work as a group or change the assignment. If the problem stems from the misbehavior of one student, take her aside, look her in the eye, and have a firm conversation.
- Try a quick fix. Sometimes something as simple as withholding a privilege or isolating the instigator will remedy the situation.
- If a real crisis erupts, don't hesitate to ask for help. Get assistance from another teacher or the school office. You will *not* be viewed as weak if you ask for help.
- Give a detention or a referral slip when negative behavior demands one.
- Never lose your composure. Sometimes, if you wait calmly, the tide may change.

Be certain that the students understand that you have classroom boundaries that may not be crossed and there will be consequences if they try to cross them. Remember, you must do everything possible to keep the classroom calm and safe.

Teacher Note

It was mid-morning and Melinda Jankowski, a full-time fifth-grade teacher at Martinville School, walked into the teachers' lounge with a scowl on her face. Her friend and colleague Terrell Farmer sat at the lunch table drinking coffee and grading papers.

He looked up and greeted Melinda, "Feeling better today? You were out yesterday, weren't you?"

"Yeah, but sometimes I think I should just come in sick. It's not worth it."

Terrell looked confused. "What's not worth it?"

"I hate coming in after being out sick to a list of problems and complaints. The sub in my room yesterday, you know, Ms. Wilson, always does this to me! Now I have to call two sets of parents, and I have to write up a referral."

Terrell commiserated. "I know what you mean. The last time I was out I came back and my desk was a mess. I couldn't find my attendance folder. My classroom library was no longer organized by categories. It took me an hour to get my room back to where it should have been."

Melinda nodded and continued her rant. "And as if that wasn't enough, when Ms. Wilson finished the story I assigned in the reading text, she went on and read the next one. I had planned to spend the whole week on the current story. I wanted to do a story map, a Venn diagram of character traits, and literature circles. She rushed ahead and advanced the curriculum. She threw off my timing completely!"

Melinda plopped down in a chair at the far end of the table. "I'm telling you, Terrell, it's not worth staying out for a day! Subs are more trouble than they're worth."

Terrell shrugged. "Not all of them. Linda Fernandez is excellent. She can sub in my room anytime. She always leaves things in better shape than she found them. And she never fails to leave a short note, so I know exactly what she covered that day. She's really good!"

Melinda frowned. "Maybe, but right now, don't talk to me about subs."

Conversations like the one between Melinda and Terrell occur every day in schools all over the country. What does it tell you? First, your job as a substitute teacher has many facets, and one of those is the way you communicate with the regular classroom teacher and the degree to which you follow the regular teacher's plan. Second, the last thing a full-time teacher wants is a list of complaints (about students, materials, or anything else). Third, your job is not only to teach the class, but also to ensure that the full-time teacher's return is as smooth as possible.

In many cases, you'll never meet the classroom teacher in person. Your primary mode of communication will be through the teacher note. And that's what we'll discuss in this chapter.

What kind of note should I write?

When you reach the end of your school day, *always* leave a note for the regular classroom teacher. The purpose of the note is to inform the teacher about what happened during the day and what needs to be done for follow-up. It has been my experience (as a full-time classroom teacher and as a sub) that the best notes are short, positive, and informative.

When the regular teacher returns to his classroom, there are many things to do and not enough time to do them before the first student walks in the door. For that reason, try to keep the note fairly short—no more than one or one and a half pages. Above all, keep your comments clear and concise, with a focus on major issues rather than minutia.

It's a good idea to start with a compliment, followed by a description of the good things that happened during the day. Any true catastrophes can be noted and minimized *after* your positive statements are made.

Each classroom teacher takes pride in his students, no matter how difficult they are. He is proud of his classroom layout and the books and tools that are available for learning. When you criticize the behavior of the class or criticize the learning environment (particularly if you do it stridently and often), you insult that teacher. Try to find the right positive words to describe your day, even if the words are putting a good spin on a generally difficult day.

Be sure to be informative by letting the teacher know which content areas you covered and what topics you were not able to present. If students had a hard time understanding a concept or couldn't complete an assignment, be sure to note that. If all material was completed, state that as well. If the classroom teacher left a plan that contained a list of "to-do" items for you to complete, it's a really good idea to put a check next to each item that was completed.

Before you sign your note, convey your willingness to talk if necessary. "If you have any questions, please don't hesitate to call me at 555-1234 or e-mail at myname@domainname.com."

And if you enjoyed your day, be sure to indicate that you'd be happy to sub in that classroom again.

What are some examples of good teacher notes?

The actual teacher note that you write should be customized to reflect your subbing experience on that day. However, it may be helpful to see some typical notes. An example of a positive note for a truly great day would be:

Mrs. Brady,

Thank you for leaving such detailed plans for me. Your students were very cooperative and helpful. I just love your class! I left you a list of the children who were especially helpful.

We completed all the material in your plans and even had some extra time. I read the children the *Arthur* book as a reward for their excellent behavior.

We really had a great day!

If you have any questions I can be reached at 555-1234. If you need a sub in the future, please ask for me.

Thanks,

Holly Haase

An example of a positive note for an unpleasant day might be:

Mr. Franks,

I hope you are feeling better. Thanks for preparing a good set of plans. They were helpful.

In general we had a good day. We covered most of the work; however, the students did not finish the math assignment. I left those papers on your desk.

You have some great students. Tiffany and Esteban were particularly helpful. We did have a few problems, but we tried to iron them out. Anthony, Enrique, and Keisha had some trouble staying focused.

If you have any questions, I can be reached at 555-1234 or andrea@domainname.com.

Thanks,

Andrea Homan

How can I improve?

Dear Barbara,

I know that I can improve my teaching skills, but I'm really not sure how to go about it. Eventually, I want to go back to college and obtain my teaching degree. For financial reasons, I can't do that right now.

There are a few experienced teachers that I have seen while I've been subbing, and they look miserable. They're always angry and perhaps they're "burnt out." I never want to be like that. I've seen others who are happy and positive. Children love them. I want to get better as time goes on, not worse.

Please give me some suggestions for improvement.

Lindsey in Nevada

Dear Lindsey,

It's very admirable that you want to improve yourself. That tells me that you will be a fine teacher someday, and you are probably a great sub already!

You're right, through time some experienced teachers develop a negative approach to teaching. They always look unhappy, and so do their students. By observing both good and bad teachers, you will start to understand what works and what doesn't.

You will find that your skills will improve greatly by subbing. When something really works in the classroom—a "great teaching moment"—repeat it until it becomes a natural part of your repertoire. Observe how the best classrooms are organized. Then borrow the best ideas and use them to make yourself a better teacher.

Find a teacher you admire and ask if you might observe him or her when you have a free period. Observe as many teachers as possible. Each one has a unique style.

Read books on teaching. Use them. You will always get inspiration and confidence from good reading materials.

Most of all, be yourself and be the very best that you can be. The more effort you put into subbing, the more you will get back in terms of fulfillment and personal satisfaction.

Both of these teacher notes are brief and to the point. In some cases, it may be necessary to describe specific situations or to indicate areas of accomplishment or problems that were encountered. However, be sure to keep the teacher note as short as possible.

Are there any statements that I should avoid in my note?

Any written document establishes a permanent record. For this reason, even a short teacher note should be constructed to reflect well on both you and the classroom teacher. With this in mind, it's a good idea to follow these guidelines as you construct the teacher note:

- **Write with humility.** Never give the permanent teacher suggestions or tell him or her what you would do in a particular situation. This is simply not your place.
- **Avoid sounding "whiny."** If you had a hard day, remember that for you it was just one bad day. The permanent teacher must face these difficult students daily.
- **Be sure *not* to include information that is confidential.** You can't be sure who else might see your note and what they might do with the information in it. If you feel uneasy about including a statement or comment about a child, leave it out of your note.

In general, your note should report, not editorialize. Avoid expressing an opinion, particularly if it reflects negatively on the class or the teacher.

Should I fill out a substitute teacher report form?

Many teachers leave substitute (sub) folders that include a Substitute Teacher Report Form for you to fill out. It's been my experience that these forms tend to be superficial and generic, but if one is provided, fill it out. However, be sure to add your own personal comments to the form and add your own note. The form usually looks something like this:

Substitute Teacher Class Report

Substitute Teacher _____ Date _____

Regular Teacher _____ Grade _____

Students Absent _____

The class: (check all that apply)

__ Followed rules

__ Was courteous and helpful

__ Worked hard on assignments

__ Other (please explain) _____

The following students:

__ Were helpful _____

 (explain) _____

__ Did something special _____

 (explain) _____

__ Were disruptive _____

 (explain) _____

The lesson plans were:

__ Completed

__ Not Completed

The assignments we did not complete were: _____

_____

_____

Comments: _____

_____

_____

_____

_____

_____

_____

_____

What else should I do at the end of the day?

After your note is written, be sure to clean the board, straighten up the teacher's desk (try to leave it as you found it), and pick items up off the floor. Usually students will be more than happy to help you with this. Straighten up the student desks also. Most schools like to have the chairs up so that the custodian can sweep the floor easily. Leaving the room in good order is your way of showing that you respect that classroom.

Summary

After you've completed a day of substitute teaching, it's only natural to be tired. But before you call it quits for the day, it's imperative that you take the time to write a teacher note. The teacher note is probably the only way that you'll actually communicate with the regular classroom teacher, and for that reason, it's important that you write it with care. The following guidelines will help:

- Keep your note brief, informative, and positive. Focus on your overall impressions for the day and note any major issues. Always try to begin with a positive comment.
- Indicate what you've accomplished. You should note which planned activities were completed and which were not. Be sure to write about any problems with academic subjects that may necessitate reteaching or reinforcement.
- Always be discreet. You never know who may glance at your note, either intentionally or by accident.
- Complete all sub forms that are provided. But be sure to add your own comments.
- Leave a clean and orderly classroom. When teachers are out for a day or longer, they prefer to come back to an orderly classroom. Leave the classroom just as the regular teacher left it. Have students help you clean the room at the end of the day.

The teacher note is a reflection on you as a professional. It's your chance to communicate with the full-time classroom teacher. It's worth spending a little bit of time and thought to do it right.

Understanding

Kristin Roberts walked down the hallway of Washington School before the opening bell, reading a text message on her cell phone. As she rounded a corner, she almost collided with another teacher, Luis Hernandez.

Luis Hernandez came to an abrupt halt, his shoes squeaking on the granite floor. He smiled.

"Hey, Kristin, who are you today?"

Kristin laughed, "I'm Mr. Brooks today."

Luis smirked. "Oh, Ken Brooks is absent again! Why is he out this time?"

"I really don't know. They don't give subs that kind of information."

Luis nodded. "If they did, you'd tell me, right?"

Kristin just smiled. "All I know is they called me this morning, and I'm happy to be a science teacher for the day."

Kristin Roberts exhibited a number of different types of *understanding* during her encounter with Mr. Hernandez in the hallway. First, she understood her role as a substitute teacher. Her job each day was, in fact, to fill in for a full-time faculty member who could not be present for one reason or another. As a replacement teacher, she understood that she had to exhibit good humor regardless of the job that was offered. As someone who appreciated the importance of ethics and privacy, she also understood that engaging in gossip ("Why is he out this time?") must be avoided, but she also understood that her interaction with other teachers should always be cordial.

In this chapter, we'll discuss a number of different aspects of *understanding* as it applies to your role as a sub.

Why is my teacher absent?

A good substitute teacher understands that students may want to know why their teacher is absent. Some are simply curious, others (particularly younger children) might be visibly upset. It's important that you address the inevitable question in a way that imparts enough information to satisfy the students' curiosity and reassures those students who might feel a bit uneasy.

As the children enter your classroom, eyes will widen when they see you.

"Where is Mr. Brooks?" one or more students might ask.

As I've noted, it's very important to take control immediately, to introduce yourself in a way that draws the class closer to you, and to have the students see you as a competent teacher and a real person. (See the Introducing Yourself chapter.) So, rather than answering the question directly, it's best to start by introducing yourself. Once that's done, you can come back to the question.

"You asked why Mr. Brooks is absent. To be honest, I'm not quite sure why he's out,[1] but I'm sure he'll be back soon. You

---

1. If you know the reason and it isn't confidential, it's perfectly acceptable to tell the class.

know, I'm very lucky to be subbing for him because everyone tells me he's a fine teacher, and I've heard good things about this class! I know we're going to have a great day, and I'll be able to give him an excellent report when he returns."

An answer like this makes everyone feel good. It satisfies natural curiosity and calms students who might be uneasy with the absence.

How and when will I understand my assignment?

In some cases you'll have plenty of time to understand your assignment. You'll get the call about your assignment in advance—sometimes days or even weeks ahead of time—e.g., when an in-service training session or a workshop has been scheduled for certain faculty members. In such cases, the teachers involved will notify the sub coordinator right away and positions are filled. More important, the classroom teacher has the time to provide you with advance notice of the topics to be covered and a good daily plan to guide you. You'll have time to gather complementary materials (if you feel it's necessary) by searching the Web for useful information. (See the Web Resources chapter.) It's an excellent idea to have a calendar or appointment book to keep track of your subbing jobs. You must be reliable, above all else.

In other situations, you'll have much less advance notice. You might get a call the evening before your assignment or even at 6:00 A.M. on the morning of the assignment. The early morning call can be jolting. It will probably wake you out of a deep sleep, so your mind and memory may not be clear. For this reason, I recommend that you keep a pencil and paper on your night table so that you can write the assignment down (school, classroom number, teacher's name). I've known more than a few subs who laughingly admitted that they forgot the school's or teacher's name after the morning call came in because they weren't quite awake. *That* can be embarrassing!

Once the call comes in and you say yes, get out of bed. It may be tempting to get five more minutes of sleep, but be careful. You certainly don't want to oversleep, and the earlier you get started, the more prepared you will be.

How can I avoid feeling like an outsider?

Let's be honest, you're not a full-time member of the school faculty, and some regulars may treat you as if you're invisible. Others, however, will be friendly and helpful. You should understand that people in any organization accept outsiders slowly (and sometimes grudgingly), and you shouldn't feel hurt if you're not immediately embraced as one of the team.

In previous chapters I emphasized the need to dress and act professionally and to engage faculty members in friendly conversation whenever you can. Remember, jeans and T-shirts are *never* appropriate for a teacher, unless the school has "dress-down day." Wearing sandals, especially flip-flops, is *not* acceptable. When I subbed, I ignored dress-down day. As a sub, I knew that I needed every trick in the book to gain respect!

Although you've done everything right, you will encounter some schools where you may get an icy reception. Don't take it personally. It's their problem, not yours!

Remember, you are an integral part of the school system, and without you (and other subs) chaos would reign. Who would take over when the teacher is out—the principal, the custodian, or the front office secretary? I doubt it! More likely, your grade partner would have to combine two classes. You're providing all of these people with a very valuable service, and regardless of how you're received, you should understand that simple fact.

What's my social position in the teachers' lounge?

You should feel free to socialize with the other teachers during free time, but you must try to be sensitive to their degree of receptivity. Usually, the conversation involves talking about topical matters within the school (e.g., students, parents, faculty). Because you don't have appropriate context, you may not know what's going on. Be a good listener and understand that it's better to be silent than to offer an opinion that is inappropriate because you don't understand the context (or the local politics).

It's a good idea to be known as a person who is understanding. Listen carefully and try to reflect feeling. If another teacher does engage you in conversation, avoid judgmental comments and allow the full-time faculty member to guide the flow of the discussion.

In the Ethics chapter I emphasized the importance of avoiding negative or "gossipy" conversations. If you become known as a gossip or align yourself with faculty members who are known as gossips, you may not be asked to return for other assignments.

How can I understand the dynamics in the classroom?

A good substitute teacher is an astute observer of human interaction. Understanding the roles of various students in the classroom and being able to identify the students who play those roles will help you immeasurably as you work to manage the class.

During your first fifteen minutes in the classroom, try to identify which students are leaders, which are followers, who is the class clown, who you can count on to be your special helper, and who you may need to protect from harassment. Watch and observe, and then use that information to be a more effective substitute teacher. (See the Classroom Management chapter.)

It's important to understand that developing observational skills takes time. Your intent is to look for patterns of behavior and then to associate these patterns with various classroom roles. Look for these personality types. I suspect you may know some of these people from your own school experience.

- **Class clown.** He loves to be the center of attention. He is often very bright, although he may struggle academically

Nagging and negative—how can I change?

Dear Barbara,

I had an awful day today. The fourth graders filed in at 7:45. I was sitting at the desk, and the students walked right up to me and started asking for special favors. They asked me to solve disagreements, even before the day began!

I found myself pleading for quiet, yelling, and nagging all day long. I know this never works, but for some reason I was in a bad mood and had very little patience for the children.

I hate being that way. How can I avoid acting like a mean person? It's not who I am, and it's not who I want to be.

Mollie in Davie, Florida

Dear Mollie,

It's a terrible feeling to be out of control. I'm glad you recognized that your methods weren't effective.

First of all, when students arrive, you should try to stand near the door and greet them one by one. Do not sit at your desk. This shows a lack of interest. Try to walk around the room while students are doing morning work and make a connection with each one. You need to show that you have a genuine interest in your students and that you want to get to know them.

Try to state all directions in a positive manner. Instead of saying, "stop talking," tell them that you would like to have all eyes on you right now because you will be giving directions. Thank them for listening. Point out those who are listening, rather than those who are not. You will create positive role models. Students will see that you notice and reward good behavior, as opposed to dwelling on the negative. When all you do is point out poor behavior, you actually give the misbehaving students your attention, which may be exactly what they want!

If you find yourself becoming negative, stop, wait a moment, and look for one good thing that is happening in the room. Comment on it, give a compliment, and move on. You'll be surprised at how you'll turn things around.

because of attention problems or learning disabilities. If you get him on your side using your own sense of humor, he will not be a problem. Be aware of his need for attention and feed into it in a positive way. Don't get too serious here. Use your own sense of humor, and you can easily outsmart this student. Appreciate him for who he is, and he will thrive on it.

- **The victim.** This student loves to say, "It's not fair!" She feels as if you are picking on her. A good approach for this student is to have a private, one-on-one conversation, without being confrontational. Explain that life's not always fair. Try to make her feel appreciated for her talents. Use a compliment to defuse the situation. "Thank you for understanding. I know this isn't easy for you. I really appreciate your cooperation."

- **The mean girl.** We all know the type. She is very pretty but actually quite insecure. She uses her ability to put down others to maintain her status in the classroom. Others are afraid to challenge her. Be careful. She has power. If you need to speak to her, do so privately. If you can get her on your side early in the day, she can be a good ally. Learn her name and establish rapport.

- **The mean boy.** He is often physically mature and gains stature by intimidating other students. He will have sycophants, but many of the students will try to avoid him. At the first sign of intimidation, you should have a private conversation. Looking him right in the eye, indicate that intimidating behavior is unacceptable, but then change course. Tell him that he could be a class leader, and you'll need his help. As with the mean girl, get him on your side early in the day and his aggressive behavior should stop.

- **The outcast.** This student appears to have a "kick me" sign on his back. He lacks social skills, and others love to get him upset. Somehow he brings out the ugly side of human nature. You will need to defend him, but don't be caught in his trap. Be sensitive, but detached if you need to be. Your overall responsibility must be to the entire group.

- **The helpful child.** This student wants your approval. She wants to be your helper. It's a pleasure to have this student on your side. Her help is needed, so why not take advantage? Everyone wins.
- **The smart one.** Usually the brightest students are high achievers and are respected by the group. However, if they lack social skills and try to flaunt their abilities, they may need to be protected from certain classmates who might not appreciate their talents.
- **The leader.** She will be a well-balanced, good student who has the respect of her peers. She has excellent social instincts and knows how to persuade others. Be sure to cultivate her help. Learn her name and call on her often.
- **The needy one.** He will want to tell you his life story, in real time! Because he wants to monopolize all of your time, you must limit your interaction with him, or you will find yourself ignoring the others. See more about the needy student later in this chapter.

A classroom is a microcosm of our society, and it's not unusual to encounter each of these student types in a classroom. Observe the class dynamic. As you gain more classroom experience, you'll learn how to identify and interact with these students. By managing the different types, you make your own day easier and the classroom much more manageable.

How can I develop a reputation as an "understanding" teacher?

If you listen to what students say (and to what they really mean), if you treat each student with respect, if you use kindness in your interactions with them, if you are firm but fair when the need arises, you'll develop a reputation as an understanding teacher.

It's not uncommon for some students to say, "I wish you were our regular teacher, you are so much nicer than Ms. X." *Never* get into a discussion of this nature. Just say, "I know that Ms. X is a fine teacher. I like her very much. And thank you for the compliment. But remember, it's easy for me to be nice, I'm only here for one day. Ms. X has to be more serious. She is responsible for your entire education this year."

As your image as an understanding teacher grows, you'll undoubtedly encounter a special student who wants your undivided attention. These "needy" children are sometimes ostracized by their peers and feel a sense of security when they are with you. Their stories can take up half of your day if you let them!

Be kind but firm. "Samantha, I'd love to talk some more, but I have to finish this note to Principal Saunders. Why don't we continue this conversation at recess?"

If you're kind and understanding, you may encounter a situation in which a student reveals sensitive information that must be considered confidential. If you learn of a situation that may be dangerous to the child, to you, or to the school, alert the principal *immediately*.

How can I be sure that the children understand what I have taught them?

Good teachers check for understanding regularly, using solid questioning techniques to ensure that students have grasped important concepts. As you pose a question, be sure that hands are raised and determine from the answers if students understand the material. (See the Questioning Techniques chapter.)

As students do independent work, circulate around the room and look at their papers to be sure that all students are doing the work correctly. Some children are embarrassed to ask for help. You should be sure to include *guided practice* during your lessons. That is, you pose a problem and the entire class works together as you guide them toward the correct solution.

In general, a substitute teacher need not worry about assessment—a job normally reserved for the full-time classroom teacher. However, if you find yourself accepting a long-term assignment, assessment will become something that you should understand and apply.

Assessment is usually accomplished in a uniform manner on grade level. Your students' textbooks will almost always provide end-of-chapter tests. In addition to these, be sure to give quizzes periodically to check for understanding. If students are not scoring well, be sure to concentrate on areas of uncertainty and reteach when necessary.

Rubrics are an effective and popular form of assessment, particularly for writing projects. They are clear statements of expectations for student work and use grading that involves a simple number system.

Funderstanding is a website that provides a more comprehensive approach, called *authentic assessment* (funderstanding .com/authentic_assessment.cfm). The authors of the site define the key goals of authentic assessment as:

- Requires students to develop responses rather than select from predetermined options
- Elicits higher-order thinking in addition to basic skills
- Directly evaluates holistic projects
- Synthesizes with classroom instruction
- Uses samples of student work (portfolios) collected during an extended time period
- Stems from clear criteria made known to students
- Allows for the possibility of multiple human judgments
- Relates more closely to classroom learning

Before you commit to a specific form of assessment, be certain to check with your grade level partners to ensure that you are all performing assessment in a consistent manner.

How can I give directions effectively for maximum understanding?

Every teacher has encountered the following sequence of events: (1) you give the students a "clear" set of directions, (2) you ask whether everyone understands, (3) everyone says they do, (4) the work begins, (5) within thirty seconds, questions arise that indicate that the students didn't understand the directions, or worse, no questions are asked and the students do the wrong thing. You will hear the dreaded, *"I don't get it."* In order to avoid this sequence, let me repeat three suggestions I made earlier:

1. State your directions clearly, *one time only*. State them when you have all the students listening. *Do not* repeat yourself. If students are used to you repeating things, they will tune out, knowing that you will say it again.
2. Write the directions on the board, so that if they say, "I don't know what to do," you can simply point to the board.
3. Ask a student to restate the directions to the rest of the class. Once students know you will do this, they will pay greater attention.

Although these guidelines do not guarantee understanding, they will force your student to *listen*, and listening is the key to understanding directions.

Summary

A substitute teacher must understand his or her own role within the classroom and the school, the dynamic among students in the classroom, the needs of each child, and the degree to which the students have assimilated the directions that have been given and the content that has been taught. To aid in this understanding, follow these guidelines:

- Understand your role within the school community. As a sub, you have an important role to play. As a contributing member of the faculty team, be responsible, be professional, and strive to have a positive attitude and to be a good listener.

- Learn to recognize the roles that students play. You should train yourself to understand the dynamic that occurs in your classroom. Who are the leaders and followers? Learn to use this information to your advantage.
- Work to become known as an "understanding" teacher. Listen to what students say, treat each student with respect, use kindness in your interactions with them, and be firm but fair.
- Be certain that students understand what you have taught them. Use the tools of assessment, guided practice, and good questioning techniques to ensure understanding of concepts.
- Provide clear directions and be sure they have been understood. Train your students to listen by *not* repeating directions.

As you've seen in this chapter, understanding has many faces. It's important for you to understand yourself, your colleagues, and your students. It's also important to ensure that your students understand the material that you present. If you achieve these goals, you'll become known as an "understanding" teacher—and that's something to strive for.

Voice

When Jennifer Muffet was a little girl, her mother used to look at her with a loving smile and say, "Speak up, Jennifer, you're such a smart girl. Nobody will be able to hear how smart you are!"

Jennifer would try, but the truth was she had a really soft voice.

The years passed, and Jennifer became a well-respected and very effective first-grade teacher. But her quiet voice remained.

"How do you get the kids to listen when they're noisy?" asked a colleague. "Your voice is so soft. I can't understand how they hear you."

"So you want to know my secret?" asked Jennifer in a voice that was barely above a whisper. She knew that her "secret" worked. All of the parents at Palm Grove School spoke highly of her, and the students adored her. She ran an orderly and calm classroom that was very conducive to learning.

Her colleague nodded.

"It's simple," said Jennifer. "At first I tried to raise my voice, but that was hopeless." She laughed. "So I tried an experiment."

"You screamed!" joked the colleague.

"No, actually the louder the children became, the softer I spoke. I would pause and say absolutely nothing. When they began to notice that I was waiting, I'd speak in a very soft voice. The children had to strain to hear me. If a few students were noisy, the others would 'shhhh' them so that they could hear what I was saying."

"But what if they didn't settle down?" asked the colleague, somewhat taken back by Jennifer's tactics.

"I'd stand in front of the class with my 'I'm waiting' look," Jennifer demonstrated for her friend. "The class would quiet down. And once they were quiet, I would continue to wait, for effect. When I finally spoke, I would calmly say, 'Thank you boys and girls.' You could hear a pin drop!"

Throughout this book, I've tried to emphasize how important it is to project confidence and control when you stand in front of a classroom. Some teachers erroneously assume that speaking in an overpoweringly loud voice will somehow indicate that they have confidence. As the story of Jennifer Muffet indicates, sometimes less is more.

Jennifer and I taught the same grade level together for years. Every time we combined classes for a special event, I was amazed at her classroom management skills. She never, and I mean *never*, raised her voice. When she needed to get her students' attention, she would turn off the lights or give a hand signal. These routines were well-rehearsed during the first few weeks of school.

Years later, Jennifer went on to become the president of the local teachers' organization where she spoke regularly in front of large groups of teachers and administrators. She always used the same technique—a long pause at the start of her presentation, followed by the use of a soft, but animated, voice. Everyone listened with great interest. Like her students, she had them in the palm of her hand!

Why is a quiet voice more effective than a loud voice?

When a teacher speaks in a soft voice, she imparts a subtle message that resides behind her words: *I'm calm and confident and don't need to raise my voice to be heard. I like my classroom to be quiet and tranquil. As a student, you'll learn that a quiet voice and a calm and tranquil demeanor will allow you to be heard and respected.*

Controlling the volume of your voice is the secret to controlling the noise level in your classroom. If you speak in a loud voice, you're broadcasting to the students that speaking loudly is acceptable to you. In fact, you subconsciously encourage it. If the teacher speaks in a loud voice, why shouldn't the students follow that lead?

When you speak softly, the children must stop their own talking or they'll miss what you are saying. To be honest, some students may not care, but the ones that do care will often do your work for you by telling the noisy students to be quiet. They want to hear you, and they'll police the classroom environment to be sure that they can.

Not everyone speaks softly. Your personality, your upbringing, and the culture that you live in all influence the way you speak. In fact, all of these factors play into the natural volume of your voice. But if you can master the art of speaking softly, you'll have a wonderful tool for teaching.

How can I tell if I am modulating my voice effectively?

Once you gain some experience, you'll learn that there's a "vibe" that you can feel when you stand in front of a group and teach. You can literally feel it when the students are tuned in to your words and when you have lost them. Their eyes, posture, and overall body language telegraph this to you.

If you're speaking in a soft voice but the vibe is *not* good, one problem might be a lack of modulation in your voice. A soft voice is calming, but a monotone puts children to sleep! Regardless of the subject matter, you must animate your words by modulating your voice. In the primary grades, it is perfectly acceptable to use a singsong voice pattern.[1] However, as your students become older, use modulation to emphasize key points and establish a rhythm for your presentation.

I tell all beginning teachers and new substitute teachers that if they think they sound too dramatic and "singsong," they are probably just about right. Use pauses, volume changes, and inflection to make your points. Your lessons will be much more interesting.

Some psychologists believe that voice articulation and modulation are nearly as important as facial expression in influencing a listener. In a set of guidelines for speakers, the U.S. Naval Academy[2] makes a number of suggestions that can be useful for subs:

- **Articulation.** People tend to judge speakers based on their ability to pronounce words correctly and clearly . . . you need to acquaint yourself with the correct method of using a dictionary to facilitate proper pronunciation.
- **Voice modulation.** Good speakers do three things with their voices to maintain audience interest.
  1. *Be enthusiastic.* This will communicate your interest and excitement for your topic and help generate audience interest, too.
  2. *Exaggerate voice inflection.* Inflection in conversational speaking is difficult to detect when you are speaking in front of an audience. Exaggerate inflection when you are making points or demonstrating some kind of emotion appropriate to the emotions that you are trying to stir in your audience.

---

1. Have you ever noticed that Kindergarten teachers are dramatic speakers? They seem to have mastered the ability to dramatically modulate their voices. Observe them in action and try to emulate their style.
2. Guidelines can be found at: http://www.usna.edu/EnglishDept/Deliver.htm.

3. *Do not speak in a monotone!* Monotone does not necessarily mean speaking in a low, droning voice. Some speakers speak in a loud monotone, and worse, some yell in monotone. You must modulate your voice (see 1 and 2 above) regardless of your speaking volume.

What's good advice for midshipmen at the U.S. Naval Academy is equally good advice for you. Try to follow it.

Is there a way that I can practice modulating my voice?

In the elementary grades, reading a story to the class is the perfect way to fine-tune your voice modulation skills. This is also an excellent way to use the *long pause* trick. Begin the story by introducing the author and illustrator. Open to the first page and just wait. Do not begin until all students are paying attention.

Read slowly for dramatic effect. Pause so that each student can absorb what has happened on the page. Let them look at the illustration. Raise your voice when appropriate, usually during dialogue when the character is loud and boisterous, and lower your voice for a quiet character.

As your voice modulation skills improve, begin using the same techniques for your own dialogue with the class.

Should I ever yell?

The answer is no, but it's only human to raise your voice at times. If you must raise your voice, do so only when you encounter *extreme* circumstances. If you do this very rarely, it will have an immediate and compelling effect on your students. When a teacher like Mrs. Muffet must raise her voice, the shock value alone will have an instantaneous effect. On the other hand, if you yell regularly, the students will become so used to it that it may not have any effect at all. Teachers who are "yellers" are usually frustrated and ineffective.

Should I ever ignore a difficult student?

Dear Barbara,

During my last subbing assignment, I had a problem student who was unable to focus and was consistently off task. When this happened, I found that it was easier to ignore him.

I know that may not be the best thing for that child, but it kept me from wasting class time, and as long as he was not disturbing the other students, it kept peace in the room.

Was I unfair to this student by ignoring him?

Adam in San Francisco

Dear Adam,

There is a delicate balance that good subs learn to achieve—the needs of one vs. the needs of all. If student X is off task, but not disturbing the others, you should finish your lesson with the class, and when you get a free moment, walk over to that student and redirect him. You may have to repeat your directions and spend some time there, but it's worth it, because you were able to continue the flow of the lesson for the group.

Another technique would be to use proximity to student X. Teach your lesson from his desk and use nonverbal signals with him. But be sure not to interrupt the flow of the lesson.

Student X may become defiant and refuse to do his work. If this happens, quietly take him aside, look him in the eyes, and tell him that he must get started. If you still experience opposition, make an arrangement. Say that you will give him a few minutes to "rest and prepare himself" and that you'll be back to check on him in a five minutes. Walk away. This usually defuses the situation.

Are there any nonverbal techniques for focusing students?

If you have to raise your voice each time you need to get students' attention, you have lost the benefits of the "soft voice" approach discussed earlier in this chapter. To avoid yelling, there are a number of nonverbal techniques that can be used.

- **Special clap.** Use a special clap to ask for instantaneous attention. Some teachers have the students imitate the clap.
- **Lights out.** Walk to the light switch and turn the light off. This is a very dramatic technique, and after a few times, just walking toward the light switch may have the desired effect.
- **Hand signals.** Most teachers raise their hand with two fingers up to indicate a need for attention. Students mimic the signal to show that they are ready to listen.
- **Props.** In the primary grades, you can use a bell and teach the children to "freeze" when the bell rings.

As a sub, you should try to determine the technique that is used by the regular teacher. Ask the special helper how the classroom teacher quiets down his or her noisy class. The students will be surprised that you know the special technique used by their teacher and will respond positively to its use.

If the classroom teacher does not have a nonverbal method for getting attention, then teach the students your own favorite method. Practice it with them and reward those who cooperate.

Summary

To be effective as a teacher, you must use your voice to project confidence and control when you stand in front of a classroom. The following guidelines will help you:

- Speak softly. Try to master the art of decreasing the volume of your voice as the student volume increases. It is a very effective tool for classroom management.
- Don't yell. Teachers who yell are out of control. Students tune them out.

- Modulate your voice. Be careful that you do not speak in a monotone. Use modulation and articulation to emphasize key points and to maintain student attention.
- Use nonverbal techniques to get the attention of the class. These techniques include lights out, a special clap, a bell or whistle, and a hand signal. Try to use the technique that is used by the regular teacher in the class because the students are already familiar with it.

Throughout this book I've implied that teachers are "actors." No one ever won an Academy Award by yelling in a monotone! The best teachers are rewarded when they use a soft, modulated, and animated voice to control their students.

Web Resources

When Justin Miller's mom used to say he had teaching in his blood, she wasn't kidding. Justin's great-grandmother taught in a one-room schoolhouse in the 1920s and 1930s. His grandmother and mother were both classroom teachers. And in less than fourteen months, Justin would graduate from Florida Atlantic University with a teaching degree.

In his junior year as an education major, Justin had enrolled in a special substitute teaching program at the university. On days when he didn't have classes, he subbed at elementary and middle schools, getting valuable classroom experience and a daily stipend that helped with school expenses. To save money, he lived at home.

Justin got home after a day of subbing to find that his grandmother was visiting.

She looked up as he walked in the door. "Justin! How's my favorite grandson?"

"Fine, Gram. How are you doing?" he said, as he walked to the refrigerator and took out a large bottle of water.

Justin's grandmother was sitting at the kitchen table, sipping tea and talking with his mother. Gram waved her hand dismissively.

"Never mind me," she said with a smile. "How did your day at school go?"

"Really well, actually. Mrs. Fernandez—she's the principal—stopped me in the hall and asked whether I could sub for two straight weeks to cover for the science teacher. He has a family emergency or something."

Justin's mother interrupted, "That's great, honey, when?"

"Beginning tomorrow—we're on break at the university, so it's no big thing, schedule-wise. But I have to teach science." Justin paused with a pensive look on his face and then said, "Mrs. Fernandez told me they're doing a unit on rocks and minerals, and I'm clueless."

"And you have to teach this tomorrow?" asked Justin's grandmother incredulously.

"Yeah. Tomorrow."

"Well, you'll have to go to the library and get some books. Lisa, do you have any science materials Justin can use? Maybe I can dig out some old stuff."

Justin smiled and raised his hand. "Gram, it's cool."

"Cool? You have to teach geology tomorrow! You need to prepare."

"I will. It'll be easy," Justin said as he walked toward the living room.

His grandmother frowned. "You're going to watch TV?"

"Yeah, Gram, I have to watch Sports Center on ESPN, and then I'll get on the Web and . . . "

Justin's grandmother continued to frown. "The Web . . . that's all I hear today . . . the Web. Whatever happened to the library, to books?"

Justin smiled. "I'll be visiting the biggest library of teacher materials on the planet, Gram. That's what the Web is, you know. I'll be ready for tomorrow. Count on it."

Justin disappeared into the living room. His mom looked at her mother, smiled, and lifted both palms skyward.

The World Wide Web is truly a wonderful teacher resource. With little more than a Google search, you'll be able to get free resources that can make the difference between a successful day of subbing and a day of struggle. When you have advance notice for a subbing assignment, try to contact the teacher you'll be subbing for and find out the subject areas to be covered. You can educate yourself first and gather useful, creative materials to enhance your lessons. Use the Web to fill your bag of tricks, to supplement the classroom teacher's plan, and to fill extra time when your lessons finish early. But above all, use it!

How do I search for teacher resources?

Everyone thinks they know how to do effective Web searches, but many people look only one layer deep on the Web. That's a mistake.

You begin, of course, with a search engine (e.g., Google or Ask.com), using keywords that seem appropriate. For example, Justin Miller might search on the following string: "Teacher resources" + science + rocks + minerals. Google returns tens of thousands of hits on the above search. You might look at the number in horror, but then you realize that the first twenty or thirty Google hits may very well provide you with more information than you could possibly need.

Beginning with the first page of references, you'll look for one or more potentially useful sites. Click through to the site and get a general feel for the material contained within it. If the resources have merit, go deeper. Look for additional links to other sites and navigate to them. Bookmark those that have useful information and go even another layer deeper, looking for still other links. Before you know it, you'll have dozens of useful age- and grade-appropriate worksheets, pictures, games, and simple experiments that you can use in any science unit on rocks and minerals.

By navigating deeper than one page, you will build a network of information that can provide immediate benefit for a one-hour lesson or a two-week unit. You can educate yourself (if you're "clueless") and use the materials you've taken off the Web to supplement curriculum content where appropriate.

Do I have to get permission to use Web resources?

In general, the answer is no. Most Web-based resources are provided to the teaching community free of charge. As long as you use them for your classroom and not for commercial purposes (i.e., you don't sell them), there is no need to get formal permission.

Can you suggest some resources to get me started?

There are literally tens of thousands of websites that cater to the needs of teachers. Some focus specifically on substitute teaching, but the vast majority address the needs of all classroom teachers (that includes you!).

In the sections that follow, I list a tiny subset of Web-based resources to give you a starting point. It's important to note that websites come and go, and their persistence is not always an indication of their quality. For this reason, I can't guarantee that the website addresses listed in this chapter will be available when you read this book. So if an interesting site is no longer active, don't despair. Another resource will always be there for your use.

The website that accompanies this book contains active links to all of the sites noted in this chapter as well as new links that will be added after the book has been published. Please visit at substituteteachingatoz.com.

Are there websites designed specifically for substitute teachers?

There are websites designed specifically for just about everything, and substitute teaching is no exception. Here are a few sites to get you started:

Substitute Teaching Institute
sti.usu.edu

This site provides a comprehensive collection of resources and advice for substitute teachers. Useful tools enable you to "identify your strengths and weaknesses prior to entering the classroom" by providing pretests followed by structured training.

Melissa's Myriad Tips for Substitute Teachers
geocities.com/athens/8020/subtips.html

A teacher shares help and hints for substitute teachers. This is a helpful and very personal website with real advice and pointers for various aspects of your subbing day.

Teachers.net
teachers.net/mentors/substitute_teaching

At this site, you can find a chat room for substitute teachers as well as advice and support.

National Education Association (NEA)
nea.org/tips/relate/subs.html

The NEA presents many suggestions that help classroom teachers prepare for a sub. It also presents helpful tips on classroom management.

A to Z Teacher Stuff
atozteacherstuff.com/tips/substitute_teaching

You will find many teacher-tested tips and a chat room. I find that the best ideas come from your fellow teachers.

Education World Magazine
education-world.com/a_curr/curr359.shtml
This site provides archives from *Education World* magazine that are particularly appropriate for your bag of tricks. It also has a joke of the day pointer, a great way to warm up your class or for use as a filler.

Guest Teacher Tips
guest-teacher.com/forums/guest-teacher-tips.php
This site offers tips on how to avoid the typical pitfalls of subbing, such as how to deal with students changing seats during attendance. Real subs give pragmatic advice that has been successful for them. Feel free to add your own!

The Substitute Teacher Home Page
csrnet.org/csrnet/substitute
This site is loaded with survival tips and helpful pointers to Web pages with word of the day, reader's theater ideas, good quotes, journal entries, and more!

Substitute Teaching—Tricks of the Trade
qnet.com/~rsturgn/index.htm
I like the personal approach presented by the author of this site. He is an experienced sub, and he wants to share his knowledge with you.

Guidelines for New and Substitute Teachers
www1.broward.edu/~nestes/newteacher.html
Prepared by the Broward County (of Florida) School Board, this site presents useful guidelines and suggestions for beginners.

Are resources designed for full-time classroom teachers appropriate for me?

In the vast majority of cases, the answer is yes. As a sub, you won't become involved in curriculum development, and, unless

How do I make a good first impression?

Dear Barbara,

I have been asked to sub in a new school. I hear it's a wonderful school, and if they like me, I'm hoping to be a regular there. I really want to make a good impression.

Any suggestions on how to start off on the right foot?

Cindy in Chicago

Dear Cindy,

I'm happy to see that you are conscious of first impressions. People make snap judgments about others, especially in a work environment. So do your best to make that first impression a good one.

Dress professionally and appropriately. Take time the night before to prepare your clothing for the next day. When you show that you care enough about yourself to dress well, others will respect you for it.

Harry and Rosemary Wong's book *The First Days of School* contains a powerful quote that has had a great impact on my career. "A professional woman should dress at least two steps above her current position. You do not dress where you are, you dress where you want to be."

When you walk into the school, introduce yourself at the office with a smile and a handshake. Find your room and write your name and the date on the board. Greet your students at the door. When class begins, take time to introduce yourself. Be sure to tell the students some personal things about yourself and tell them you hope to learn about them as the day goes on.

At the end of the day, leave the room clean and neat. Write an upbeat teacher note. Say good-bye to the office staff. Tell them what a delightful day you have had and that you hope to be back again soon.

My guess is that you'll be asked back as soon as a sub is needed.

you land a long-term subbing assignment, you probably won't have to develop lesson plans, but much of the content from general teaching resource sites focuses on helpful materials and tips that can be used in day-to-day teaching. This information is as valuable to you as it is to any full-time classroom teacher.

In this section, I've provided a sampling of Web resources designed for full-time teachers but useful to every sub as well.

Teachnology.com
teach-nology.com
This site contains everything from lesson plans to teaching tips to games to rubrics. An excellent resource for day-to-day educational materials.

The Teacher's Corner
theteacherscorner.net
Here you can find links to a wide array of useful teacher resources with ideas for lesson plans in all subject areas, seasonal items, bulletin boards, and much more.

Time to Teach
timetoteach.co.uk
This is a resource for teachers in a hurry and very useful for the typical substitute teacher.

Harry and Rosemary Wong at Teachers.net
teachers.net/gazette/wong.html
This site presents guidelines and advice for teachers by two of the best authors in the field. This site is a good supplement to Harry and Rosemary Wong's well-respected book *The First Days of School*.

101(+) Teaching Tips
help4teachers.com/tips.htm
Dr. Kathie Nunley presents an interesting article that outlines key teaching tips.

Teaching Treasures
teachingtreasures.com.au
From the Australian site: "Parents, teachers, and students using this educational site will find many free unique teaching tools, online interactive activities, projects, worksheets, and many other resources to help with the daily educational learning adventure."

Sites for Teachers
sitesforteachers.com/index.html
An excellent portal, this site contains thousands of links that will be useful for teachers.

Teacher Planet
teacherplanet.com
This site features more than 250 theme-based resource pages organized alphabetically.

A to Z Teacher Stuff
atozteacherstuff.com
From the site: ". . . a teacher-created site designed to help teachers find online resources more quickly and easily. Find lesson plans, thematic units, teacher tips, discussion forums for teachers, downloadable teaching materials & eBooks, printable worksheets and blacklines, emergent reader books, themes, and more."

4Teachers.org
4teachers.org
This site presents useful tools and resources for teachers, including resources in Spanish.

tlsbooks.com Free Worksheets
tlsbooks.com
Here you can find hundreds of excellent worksheets for children in Kindergarten through Grade 5. Both language arts and math worksheets are presented.

Teacher Talk Classroom Management Questionnaire
   education.indiana.edu/cas/tt/v1i2/what.html
   This site contains a simple questionnaire that will provide
   you with a feel for your "classroom management profile."

Are there specialized resources for curriculum areas such as math or social studies?

Absolutely! No matter how obscure the curriculum area, it's
almost certain to have many websites dedicated to it. In this
section I'll provide you with a few links to websites dedicated
to math, science, language arts, social studies, technology,
graphic arts, music, and "for fun."

Math Resources

Math Is Fun
   mathsisfun.com
   This excellent math teaching resource includes games, puzzles, and tools for all levels of math instruction. It contains
   dozens of useful links to other math sites.

Math Excellence
   ct4me.net
   A wide variety of information for math teachers can be
   found here.

MathsforKids
   mathsforkids.com
   Practice is provided in elementary math and geometry as
   well as more advanced math topics.

Multiplication.com
   multiplication.com
   Here you will find everything you need for teaching
   multiplication.

Math Sense
mrspohlmeyerskinderpage.com/mathsense.htm
A site created by a teacher who writes ". . . my collection of math ideas and activities that you can use in your classroom. I believe that teaching math through the use of literature is an excellent way to provide various experiences for young children."

Nick's Mathematical Puzzles
qbyte.org/puzzles
More than 150 *difficult* math puzzles in geometry, trigonometry, and algebra at the high school level are available here.

Science Resources

Science Mini-Lessons
youth.net/cec/cecsci/sci-elem.html
Mini-lessons for 130 different science topics designed specifically for elementary Grades K–5 are included.

Science Links
www1.broward.edu/~nestes/science.html
This site contains links to a wide variety of math and science resources, including the solar system, trees, a frog dissection, fossils, and many others.

Science Resources
softschools.com/science
Listed here are useful resources for a variety of science topics including animal classification, rain forests, rocks, earthquakes, and the human body.

Science Websites Integrated with TV Presentations
nationalgeographic.com
kids.discovery.com
discovery.com
pbs.org
pbskids.org
Each of these websites complement programming on popular television or cable networks and often have excellent resources for science learning.

Language Arts Resources

Web English Teacher
webenglishteacher.com
This site presents a wide array of language arts and literature resources.

Florida Center for Reading Research
fcrr.org/Curriculum/studentcenteractivities.htm
In-depth curriculum for topics such as phonics, fluency, vocabulary, comprehension, and others can be found here. Also included is a detailed Teacher's Guide.

Language Instruction
www1.broward.edu/~nestes/language.html
This site contains many useful pointers for language arts teachers.
www1.broward.edu/~nestes/writing%20skills.html
This website contains links to a variety of useful resources for teaching writing skills, including worksheets, document formats, and more.

Reading is FUNdamental
sandralreading.com
This site strives to improve reading comprehension skills with "educational games, card games, reading skills puzzles, plays, monthly activities, and multimedia materials;

balanced with these practice activities: reading worksheets, test preparation, struggling readers, and summer review."

English as a Second Language
eslcity.com/english
Presented here are many useful English as a second language (ESL) resources.

Stories
storiestogrowby.com
This website offers free folktales and fairy tales from around the world, as well as lesson plans to go with them.

Reading a-z.com
readinga-z.com/newfiles/preview.html
Downloads for thirty free children's books can be found at this site.

Social Studies Resources

National Council for Social Studies
ncss.org/resources
Links to dozens of resources that can be used for social studies curricula with a heavy emphasis on current events and topics.

Teaching Current Events Via Newspapers, Magazines, and TV
csun.edu/~hcedu013/cevents.html
This website offers links to all major media sources and has suggestions for using media content in teaching current events.

Social Studies for Kids
socialstudiesforkids.com
At this site, you can find useful resources across a broad range of social studies subtopics.

Technology Resources

kidsandcomputers.com
kidsandcomputers.com
This is an interactive site that will help students learn about computers and computer programs.

howstuffworks.com
howstuffworks.com
This site breaks down information into simple terms on a wide variety of topics.

Graphic Arts Resources

KidsArt
kidsart.com
Useful resources for art instruction, including study units, and hundreds of links to art projects, books, and worksheets for all grade levels, are available at this website.

Art Education Resource
picturebookart.org
This site presents useful resources for art instruction.

Art Links
mmwindowtoart.com/links.html
Links to dozens of art sites for teachers and students can be found at this website.

Music Resources

K-12 Resources for Music Educators
isd77.k12.mn.us/music/k-12music
This is a major portal for music resources.

Songs for Teachers
songs4teachers.com
More than 125 free songs for elementary grade teachers are available at this site.

"For Fun" Resources

FunBrain
funbrain.com
This site is a fun and exciting site for students to visit. It relays information through facts and games, which makes the information a little more exciting to learn.

Puzzles.com
puzzles.com
Here you can find puzzles and games for all ages as well as many links to other puzzle sites and an interesting section on puzzle projects. Many downloads are offered.

Summary

You have direct access to the largest, most comprehensive collection of teaching resources that has ever existed. It expands and improves every day and provides you with instantaneous help whether you're subbing in a Kindergarten or in a middle school science class. Here are a few guidelines for using the Web effectively:

- Learn how to do an effective Web search. Be sure to search more than one level deep, building a network of resource sites that collectively provide you with the information you'll need.
- Use the resources freely. Although much of the material is protected by intellectual property law, it is provided for your use as a teacher, free of charge.
- Get started by examining websites designed explicitly for subs. Use the list of resources provided in this chapter as

a starting point. Take advantage of chat rooms for subs. Participate in the sharing of ideas.

- Take advantage of the resources developed for full-time classroom teachers. After all, you're one of them, except for the "full-time" part.
- Recognize that specialized resources exist for all subject areas. Use the lists of resources provided in this chapter as a starting point.

If you use the Web effectively, you'll cut your preparation time substantially. You'll also add to your bag of tricks on a daily basis and become a sub known not only for your teaching skill but also for the unique and creative complementary content you present.

X-Ray Vision

Substitute teacher Shanti Shah was writing an equation on the board. She knew that something was going on in her classroom, but her students didn't know she knew. She turned and, without hesitation, walked to the back of the room. She took a note from Jamie Robertson's hand, just as he was about to pass it to his friend Michael.

"I'll take that, please," she announced.

Jamie was dumbfounded. "How did you see my note, Ms. Shah?"

"Didn't you know that all teachers have *x-ray vision*? We have eyes in back of our heads," she replied with a sly smile.

A few students laughed as Jamie pondered this new information.

Ms. Shah took the note, and without looking at it or saying another word, put it in her pocket. She walked back to the board and continued with her lesson, pleased at how smoothly her fifth-period math class was going.

When the forty-five-minute period was over, Shanti stood in the doorway and said good-bye as each of her students filed past. When Jamie arrived at the door, she asked to speak to him privately.

"Jamie, I didn't want to embarrass you by talking about the contents of your note in front of your classmates. I know you're a good kid. Just take this as a warning."

Jamie tried to interrupt. "But . . ."

Shanti put up her hand to stop her. "This isn't a debate, Jamie, and there are no 'buts.' When I'm teaching, it's serious and important business. If you're writing and passing notes, you're not paying attention, and that will only hurt you. Worse, you're distracting other students and they're not paying attention."

Jamie bowed his head slightly as Shanti continued. "I usually know what's going on, so please don't do this again. Do you understand?"

"Yes, Ms. Shah."

Jamie now knew that when Ms. Shah was subbing, she would be in charge. Yet, she was "cool" enough not to embarrass him in front of his peers. Jamie had newfound respect for Ms. Shah, and his classroom behavior would show it.

Shanti Shah could have reprimanded Jamie the moment she took the note, but in doing so, she'd lose the rhythm of her lesson and embarrass Jamie in front of his peers. Instead she coolly defused the in-class situation and then handled the reprimand privately. She exhibited something called "withitness."

What is withitness?

Like all good teachers, Shanti Shah is a multitasker. Her mind is able to process multiple sensory inputs at once—the random sounds in the classroom, the voices of her students, people walking by her classroom door—all while conducting a lesson and focusing on the educational content that needs to be presented. She displays a characteristic that educators refer to as *withitness*.

When a teacher has withitness, she seems to have x-ray vision. It's almost as if the teacher knows what's going to happen before it actually does. Withitness encompasses multitasking, classroom awareness, alertness, intuition, and confidence—all in a way that projects a powerful image to every student in the classroom. The teacher is in control. She *knows*, and because she knows, the students know that there is no need to act out. Because she *knows*, she can stop misconduct with a look. Her body language and proximity enable her to maintain control effortlessly.

In an article entitled "Are You with It?," Deb Wuest presents an excellent summary of withitness and related characteristics that all lead to effective classroom management.[1]

> *Do your students think you have "eyes behind your head"? Can you deal effectively with the demands of several students at the same time? Are you effective at maintaining lesson momentum, changing activities when interest is waning or modifying activities to keep students busy? If so, you are using many of the techniques incorporated by Kounin into his discipline model.*
>
> *Kounin's model focuses on preventive discipline—techniques and strategies designed to prevent the occurrence of discipline problems in the first place. According to Kounin, good classroom management depends on effective lesson management. Kounin's key ideas include the "ripple effect," "withitness," "overlapping," effective transitions, class management, and satiation.*

---

1. Deb Wuest's article can be found at pecentral.org/climate/april99article .html. Used by permission of PE Central (pecentral.org), the premiere site for physical education educators.

Wuest proceeds to describe two of Jacob Kounin's[2] key ideas:

Ripple Effect. *The "ripple effect" occurs when the teacher corrects a misbehavior in one student, and this positively influences the behavior of other nearby students. The ripple effect is influenced by the clarity and firmness of the correction. The effect is greater when the teacher clearly names the unacceptable behavior and gives the reasons for the desist. Firmness, that is, conveying an "I mean it" attitude, enhances the ripple effect. The ripple effect is greatest at the beginning of the year and diminishes as the year progresses. At the high school level, Kounin found that respect for the teacher along with high motivation to learn lead to the greatest student involvement and minimum misbehavior by students.*

Withitness. *"Withitness" is a term created by Kounin to describe the teacher's awareness of what is going on in all parts of the classroom at all times. We commonly refer to this as "having eyes in the back of the head." To be effective, the students must perceive that the teacher really knows what is going on in the gymnasium. If students are off task and fooling around, the teacher needs to send a clear message that communicates to the students that the teacher sees that they are not working and they need to get started. Withitness can be improved with practice, such as learning how to effectively use systematic techniques to scan the class. Keeping your "back to the wall" as you move throughout the class helps you see the broader picture and be more aware of what is going on.*

2. Kounin, J. S. *Discipline and Group Management in Classrooms.* Holt, Reinhardt and Winston, 1970. WikiEd suggests an updated treatment by Charles Wolfgang. *Solving Discipline and Classroom Management Problems: Methods and Models for Today's Teachers.* John Wiley and Sons, 2001.

The effectiveness of withitness is increased when the teacher can correctly identify the student who is the instigator of the incident. Teachers who target the wrong student for a desist or a reprimand are perceived by the students as not knowing what is really going on (i.e., not "witit"). When several incidences of misbehavior occur at the same time, it is important that teachers deal with the most serious incidence first. Timing is another aspect of withitness. Teachers should intervene early and quickly in dealing with misbehavior. Failure to do so allows the misbehavior to spread.

Both the *ripple effect* and *withitness* are important ideas. When taken together, they can help you to project an aura that leads students to believe you have x-ray vision.

How do I develop x-ray vision?

X-ray vision is, of course, just an illusion. But you can use a few simple tricks to make this illusion real for your students. For example, you notice that a student has just started some action that will lead to misbehavior (e.g., a student takes a cell phone out of her desk). Turn your back for a moment and write something on the board or adjust papers on your desk. Then, without saying a word, quietly walk over to the child. In a soft but commanding voice say, "I'd like the cell phone, Nastasha. Please give it to me."

Nastasha will look up, eyes wide. "How did you know?"

Your answer, "I know everything that happens in my classroom."

This dialogue, if handled with subtle drama, will foster the illusion that you have x-ray vision. Later, when you notice that Natasha has changed her behavior for the better, react to her in a positive way. Walk to her desk and quietly say, "Thank you, Natasha. I noticed how you are really trying to listen, and I want you to know that I appreciate it."

Stopping student misconduct using nonverbal techniques is another important way to give the illusion of x-ray vision. I was given a long-term subbing assignment in a primary classroom with an inclusion student, Justin, who had serious emotional issues. He had poor socialization skills, and his behavior was extremely disruptive.

Another child in the class, Ian, was genuinely sensitive and kind to Justin, and the two became classroom friends. I decided to ask Ian to help me handle Justin's disruptive behavior, and together we developed a strategy. Every time Justin would act out toward another student, Ian would step in and remind him that his behavior was a problem or distract him with something else. Justin respected Ian and wanted to maintain the friendship. Ian was a natural at managing Justin's volatile temper. It worked beautifully.

I rewarded Ian by giving him a special sign each time he did his "job." Our eyes would meet, and I would smile and give him a subtle thumbs-up. Ian would beam with pride.

Justin never knew our little secret, and Ian's self-esteem soared. No time was taken away from learning. No words were needed. A smile and a thumbs-up were all that were necessary.

The illusion of x-ray vision will provide you with a subtle technique for classroom management that doesn't interrupt the flow of your lesson. Effective teachers never waste time with continual nagging, repeated warnings, or engaging in unnecessary dialogue with students. Their discipline is almost invisible.

Should I use x-ray vision on the whole class or just with individuals?

The x-ray vision illusion is most effective one-on-one. Other students will notice your interaction, and it will make an impression.

Whenever possible, it is best to have personal interactions. Whole-group conversations should be kept to a minimum. In general, most students are well behaved. It's usually two or three students that are disruptive. Unfortunately, their behavior can ruin a perfectly wonderful group.

What should I do if I can't handle an unruly student?

Dear Barbara,

What should I do if I simply cannot handle a student? I hate to admit to being weak, but there are times when one student can ruin the day. Yesterday a sixth-grade girl was taunting another child, hurting her feelings in a very mean way. When I tried to stop her, she became angry and raised her arm to me.

I backed away at that point because I had a sense that I might be in danger. With time, the uncomfortable situation was defused. However, I was left with an uneasy feeling. What if this young lady really blew up and hurt me or another student?

Sue Anne in Baltimore

Dear Sue Anne,

When you sense danger, trust your instincts and ask for help. You tried your best to remedy the problem on your own, now take it one step further.

Each school has its own method for requesting help. Hopefully, there will be a PA system or a walkie-talkie. Call the office and tell them that you need assistance immediately.

If for some reason help does not arrive in time, you can ask a student to go to the teacher next door for assistance. If you are being physically threatened, the student should be removed from your class immediately.

You will not be viewed as weak. You have shown that you have self-respect and that you are a professional. Your concern for the well-being of the students in your room is your number one priority.

If you can show these individuals that you are aware of their behavior and will deal with it appropriately on a personal level, you will have good results. The ability to stop problems before they begin is the reason you want to foster the x-ray vision illusion.

Is there a "look" that can help?

Many teachers have a special look that they use to indicate that they are displeased. If the look is effective, they can continue teaching the lesson without interruption or verbal interaction. Professional educators call this "controlling behavior using a nonverbal technique." It's discipline without interrupting instruction.

In a very funny book, Phillip Done describes his methods of mastering **THE LOOK** to a student teacher that is training in his classroom.[3]

> *Every teacher has a collection of looks. You have to or you won't survive. . . . Let me explain. Basically there are five different teacher looks. The first one is called the Raised Eyebrow. It's easy. Simply raise both eyebrows as high as you can. Do not speak. Keep your head perfectly still. Stare at the child for five to ten seconds.*

Done goes on to describe all five looks and when to use them in a wonderfully comic style. The body language that you use, including your look, will be a wonderful tool for classroom management.

But please remember to use your "look" with a sense of humor. Children need to know that you are serious about your expectations for them, but they must feel that you have a human side to go along with the "look." When used properly, the "look" can defuse a tense situation.

Can x-ray vision be used to read someone's mind?

Good teachers have a way of being able to read the emotional needs of their students. You must develop a keen sense of observation to develop this sixth sense. When a student is upset, depressed, or agitated, he will provide you with a set of

---

3. Done, P. *32 Third Graders and One Class Bunny*. Touchstone, Simon & Schuster, 2005.

cues. Some are visual (e.g., hunched shoulders, head tilting downward), others are auditory (e.g., a shaky voice), and still others may be more outwardly behavioral. Through observation, you must try to sense when a student is upset and "ready to explode." Those are the times when you need to just back off. Conversely, teachers need to be able to sense when a student needs positive reinforcement and move to provide it. The same visual, auditory, and behavioral cues will help.

Just as important, good substitute teachers must know when they need to "read someone's mind." You'll know when it is necessary to intercede to avoid disruptive behavior and act appropriately to provide positive reinforcement.

To illustrate this point, I want to give you a personal example. I was subbing in a ninth-grade classroom and encountered a young lady whose academic skills were weak. To mask her weakness, she enjoyed disrupting class as an escape from doing her work. Ignoring directions was a good way to procrastinate. Defying her teacher was another pastime.

I noticed that she loved to wear jewelry (a visual cue) and she had a wonderful sense of style (or at least as wonderful as any ninth grader could have).

During an unstructured time, I decided to compliment her on her style and good taste. I took the time to have a "fashion conversation." I asked her for some shopping advice for myself. She responded well. After that, I was sure to notice her jewelry selections and comment on them whenever it seemed appropriate. Through observation, I "read her mind," found common ground, and established a communication pathway. After that, I had very little trouble with her behavior.

Summary

X-ray vision is an illusion that effective teachers use to create an "all-knowing" image. As a sub, you can do the same thing, and, as a result, you will be better able to manage your classroom. The following guidelines will help:

- Strive to achieve "withitness." A good substitute teacher is able to anticipate situations before they happen by using a combination of multitasking, classroom awareness, alertness, intuition, and confidence.
- Recognize that the "ripple effect" can serve you well. If you can correct the behavior of one student, your effort can ripple across the classroom and positively influence all students. To accomplish this, you have to clearly identify the behavior problem and address a solution firmly.
- Focus on one-to-one interactions when behavioral problems arise. If you sense that a particular student needs your attention or is misbehaving, address that student privately rather than disrupting or punishing the entire class.
- Use little tricks to establish the x-ray vision illusion. Wait a beat before you correct a misbehavior you've observed, allowing students to believe you have eyes in the back of your head. As you develop this skill, you'll learn to take advantage of the illusion.
- Use facial expressions to convey your reactions to student conduct. If you are pleased, show it. If you are displeased, you can develop your "look."
- Try to sense and anticipate the needs of individuals and address them individually with those students. Develop a repertoire of individual responses to particular students. They will appreciate your individualized attention.

Like many other aspects of effective substitute teaching, x-ray vision comes naturally for some and is a struggle for others. But with effort and practice, you too will hear a wide-eyed student ask you, "How did you know?"

Young at Heart

Christine Hammond, a twenty-year-old junior majoring in education, decided to sign up for subbing at the local middle school on the days she didn't have university classes. Her major concern was that she wasn't much older than her students.

Christine was assigned to an eighth-grade science class. Unlike some subs who are "science impaired," Christine loved the subject area and felt very comfortable with the content she had to present.

The lesson plans that were left by the regular classroom teacher were clear—the students would watch a video on the human body. Then, they were to read a chapter in the text and answer questions on a worksheet. Christine arrived at school early and had plenty of time to look over the questions on the worksheet. Two questions were new to her, so she took the time to find the answers in the text. When the eighth graders filed into the classroom, she was at the door ready to greet them.

As they took their seats, she introduced herself. "I'm Ms. Hammond, and I'll be substituting for Mr. Woods today. I'm a student at State University."

"Cool," said Amanda, a dark-haired young teen with an inquisitive expression. "That's where I want to go to college."

Christine smiled. "Really? Well, it's hard work, but you'll learn a lot and still have time for a little fun."

"What's college like?" asked a tall young man in the second row.

"Are the professors strict?" asked a girl sitting in the back of the classroom.

"Do you live on campus?" asked another student.

"Do you have a boyfriend?" asked Amanda to a chorus of giggles from the female students.

Christine seized the moment. She knew that her proximity to their age and her college student status made her an intriguing person for the eighth graders, and she answered a few questions. She ended by saying, "I'd love to talk more about college life, but we'd better get started on the *human body*. After the video, we can do the worksheet together. I'd be happy to help you with your work—after all, it wasn't too long ago that I studied this material in my eighth-grade science class! If we have time at the end of the period, I can talk to you about college life. I think you'll find it *very* interesting!"

Christine Hammond didn't have to worry about being "too young." To an eighth grader she was a woman of the world, and her background as a college student intrigued and engaged almost every student in the class.

Although you may no longer be twenty years old (sigh!), you can still be young at heart, and when you are, you'll have a better chance of engaging your students and having a successful time in the classroom.

How does age relate to successful subbing?

To children, all grown-ups are "old." Because children are not very good at judging the age of an adult, you can use your years of life experience as a helpful tool.

Regardless of your chronological age, it is important to be able to relate to the students and be cognizant of their world. You should try to make yourself aware of the media, technology, and culture of the age group with which you are working. Know what TV shows they watch, which music they listen to, which sports and teams they might enjoy. It's a good idea to drop a name of a famous singer or popular TV show. In a subtle way, it establishes credibility and indicates that you understand their world. It's also fun to see their reaction when you mention a pop icon or video game that they assume you don't know.

"Wow, Mrs. P., you actually know about Sponge Bob?" exclaimed a third grader when I mentioned the cartoon character.

"Sure," I responded (exaggerating just a little). "I watch him all the time. He's one of my favorites!"

At one point in my career, I subbed in the same school system that my children attended. I always played up my role as a mother of children "exactly your age" who attended a neighboring school that all the children knew. Some of the students actually knew my sons. This helped establish me as a teacher and a mom, just like theirs.

What if I am an older person? Will the students relate to me?

If you are an older person, you probably have had some very good life experiences to share with students. Don't be afraid to talk about them, but do try to avoid a preaching tone. Your intent is to provide a "history lesson," not to convince the children that things were better in the good old days.

I love to tell students what it was like when I was in their grade. Every child knows what "old school" means, and all are

How do I reach a quiet student?

Dear Barbara,

It seems to me that loud, outgoing students get the majority of my attention. I'm forced to learn their names immediately, and they monopolize most of my time.

In each of my classes, there are always one or two very quiet children. I rarely learn their names and worry that I inadvertently neglect them. How can I reach these quiet children?

Sara in Rhode Island

Dear Sara,

It's admirable that you have the sensitivity to be aware of that quiet boy or girl in the back of the room. Most subs are so busy keeping up with the outgoing, louder students that they forget the individuals who may really need your attention. The quiet ones are often too shy to ask for help.

Once you have attended to the obvious needs of the majority, try to walk around the room and get to know the quiet ones. Compliment them on their behavior and work. Learn their names and call on them during class discussions. Ask them to be your special helpers. Use recess time as an opportunity to have a conversation with them.

Your caring attention will have an impact on a shy student. You'll both benefit from the relationship.

fascinated with what it was like in the old days. They are often dumbfounded when I tell them that there were no calculators or computers or cell phones, no Google or video games.

"You know, boys and girls," I'd say, "when I was in the third grade . . ."

"That must have been a *long* time ago," the classroom comic would interject.

"It was," I'd say with a laugh, "but in those days school wasn't for wimps."

"Do you mean, Mrs. Pressman, it was tough?"

"Yep."

"Not tougher than here."

"When I was in third grade, we had to memorize multiplication facts and then recite them in front of the whole class, and if we made a mistake, we'd get punished."

"How?"

"You'd have to write the part of the multiplication table you didn't know twenty-five times, and you'd stay after school until you got it done!"

"Whoa! They can't do that."

"Like I said, school in the old days was not for wimps."

As I've mentioned in earlier chapters, the more students know about you and your background (and history) the better you'll be able to engage them. So tell them about your previous career, about the years you lived in a big city, about interesting family members, about your trips to far-off places—you'll be more "human."

Is it true that being "immature" helps you be a better teacher?

In my current job, I train new teachers, and I've noticed that the very best teachers are the ones who have a whimsical persona. They have the ability to be somewhat childish when they need to be.

The best teachers love to be silly. They are not afraid to use self-deprecating humor. They can get into the mind of a child and make him or her laugh.

During a job interview, I was once asked how I would feel if I were observed by parents and administrators for a special early childhood program in the school district.

My answer: "I never mind being observed. I am very happy to make a fool of myself in front of anyone who wants to watch me!"

I could tell from the laughter and warm smiles that this response got me the position. Any good teacher knows that your ability to act in a childish manner makes you an effective teacher or substitute teacher.

Summary

Your chronological age has very little to do with your effectiveness as a substitute teacher. Remember, children are interested in your age, but they will not be judgmental about it. They are fascinated by age differences. Try to apply the following guidelines:

- Stay current. Learn the current culture—media, music, and the like—and use this knowledge in the classroom. It will help establish credibility.
- Use your age as an asset. If you've very young, recognize that your students may be able to relate to your experiences because they are not too far removed from theirs. If you're older, understand that life experiences provide you with many effective teaching tools.
- Don't be afraid to be whimsical. A little "immaturity" goes a long way in the classroom.

If you stay young at heart, your chronological age really doesn't matter. Effective teaching is about the way you translate your life experience into the classroom, not about how much—or little—life experience you have.

Zoo and Other Field Trips

When the phone rang at 6:15 A.M., Anna Russell knew it was the Milford School District sub coordinator.

"Hello," Anna said, her voice still groggy.

"Hi, Anna, we have a special assignment today."

How could the sub coordinator be so cheery at 6 o'clock in the morning? thought Anna.

"We need you to sub for a fourth-grade field trip to Beardsley Zoo."

"A field trip to the zoo?" said Anna. "Uh, okay, I'll take it."

As she drove in to school an hour later, Anna began to worry. *I've never done a field trip before,* she thought. *What if a student gets sick. What if I lose a child?*

She smiled and shook her head. "Take a breath," she said out loud. "You're organized and sensible. You've worked in this school before. You can do this."

When Anna arrived at the fourth-grade classroom, she saw a list of instructions on the teacher's desk:

1. Count permission slips and send them to the office. No slip, no trip.
2. Nurse Lisa has the first-aid kit.
3. Alex's dad, Dr. King, is a chaperone. He'll handle his son's inhaler and any other medical emergency.
4. Assign students to the parent chaperones as listed on the board.
5. You'll have Brittany and Patrick in your group. You'll see why.
6. Remember to bring the envelope with the zoo entrance voucher.
7. Be sure to count heads throughout the day.

The teacher used a happy face at the end of the list rather than a signature. Anna hoped it would indeed be a happy day

As the bus pulled up to Beardsley Zoo, students walked excitedly to the entrance. A staff member met them.

"Hi, girls and boys, we're glad to have you at Beardsley Zoo. We're going to start with the reptile exhibit. Follow me."

As the class entered the area dedicated to snakes, Anna noticed Patrick, a small blond headed boy, pulling back, looking around with fear in his eyes. As the zookeeper held a snake to show the students, Patrick cowered in the corner, frozen in panic. He looked as if he would cry.

Brittany snickered, "Scared, Patrick? What a baby!"

Anna knelt down and quietly whispered, "We all have fears, Patrick. Sometimes we're afraid of the unknown."

"I'm not afraid," said Patrick as his lower lip quivered. "It's just . . . I don't like snakes . . . that's all."

Anna smiled empathetically. "You know, Patrick, I don't like 'em much myself. I'll bet neither one of us has been this close to a snake before."

Patrick nodded but still held back.

Anna put her hand on his shoulder. "I'm going to ask you to take your fear and put it in a special box. I'm going to take that box and hold it for you. You can have it back later if you need it. For now, let's just listen and learn together."

She pantomimed opening a box lid and then closing it. Patrick smiled, just a little.

"This snake," said the zookeeper, "is a spotted python. It grows to five feet and eats little frogs, lizards, and bats."

Students listened to the facts with great interest. As the zookeeper talked, Patrick slowly moved closer. When the presentation was complete, students filed out. Patrick slowly approached the zookeeper. "Can I touch the python?"

The zookeeper smiled. "Sure!"

Anna and Patrick exchanged knowing glances. "I guess you won't be needing that box back, Patrick."

Patrick smiled broadly. "You can keep it, Ms. Russell."

Throughout this book, I've emphasized that a good sub must be ready for anything. Whether you're off to the zoo, the local science museum, or a play at the local university, a class trip makes significant demands on every teacher who participates. The safety of the children is your responsibility. Their good (or bad) behavior in public reflects on both you and the school. The parents who attend as chaperones can be a great help, but in their own way, they need to be managed in much the same way as the children do.

A day outside the confines of the school building can be fun, but only if you know what to do, how to handle the responsibility, and how you'll need to prepare. In this chapter I'll try to provide you with some guidance in each of these areas.

What type of trip should I expect?

The easiest field trips to manage are those that go to an entertainment or cultural venue such as a theater, ballet, concert, or opera. The students are seated in an auditorium, monitoring is relatively easy, and their movement is constrained. Trips that take the children to an outdoor venue—zoos, theme parks, and beaches, to name just a few—with many potential attractions are probably more fun for the children, but they can pose significant challenges for the teacher and the parent chaperones.

If your class is going to an entertainment or cultural venue, it's a good idea to provide some background or context before the trip, so that the students understand the things they will see and hear. It's also very important to have the students recognize that their behavior will be very important and will be monitored carefully.

If the class is going to an outdoor venue, it is critical to establish tracking techniques, assign a buddy system, define meeting times, establish groups with assigned chaperones, and specify other safety procedures. It's also very important to provide name tags identifying the child, the school, and the location of the transportation.

What do I need to know about permission slips?

Virtually every school system demands formal parental permission for all out-of-school activities (and some that occur in school). Therefore, every child who will be going on the field trip *must* have a signed permission slip. No slip, no trip!

In most cases, slips are sent home a few weeks before the trip and are collected in the days immediately preceding the trip. If the slips are not in the classroom (check the teacher's desk), be certain to check in the school office. Compare the list of students against signed slips. If a child does not have the permission slip, the office staff will try to contact the parent. If this is not possible, they will arrange to have the student sit in another classroom for the day.

Should I divide the children into groups?

If you're going on an outdoor field trip, it is critically important to divide the children into small groups and assign one or more parent chaperones and/or teachers to each group. Although there is no ideal group size, I have found that groups of four or five children are manageable and safe.

Children like to be with their friends, so try to keep friends together when defining groups. If you don't know what friendships exist, I've found that it's a good idea to work with a trusted student when dividing into groups. Assign groups in private. Do not allow too much class input. (Begging may occur!) If a parent chaperone has a child in the class, be sure to assign that child to the parent's group.

Sadly, one or two children may not be wanted in anyone's group. Be sensitive to this. Although you could force the issue, it's probably better (for the child) not to insist that he or she be included with other children who might torment or be mean to that student. I always kept the "unwanted" child with me, along with a "popular" child. This gives the "unwanted" child some status. In addition, if there is a particularly difficult child, be certain that student stays with you.

How can I get the most help from parent chaperones?

Usually the parents who go on the trips are the room mothers or fathers and are active PTA members. They will be extremely helpful and will probably know the children better than you do. In order to get the most from your chaperones, I would suggest the following guidelines:

- Share cell phone numbers so that you can stay in touch throughout the day.
- Go over safety rules.
- Review special health precautions for individual students.
- Have parents help you keep track of students by "counting heads" often.

What should I be certain to bring?

Many classroom teachers put all necessary field trip information and materials (such as tickets or vouchers) into a large envelope or folder. If you don't find one, ask. But even if an

How should I handle an angry parent?

Dear Barbara,

Today an angry parent walked into my room as the students were filing out for dismissal. She was clearly upset and got right "in my face" to tell me that I had better stop picking on her son.

To be honest, I wasn't sure what she was talking about, but it was obvious that she was agitated and concerned.

I asked her to please wait until I dismissed the children. Then we sat down. She claimed that I had blamed her son, Tyson, for starting a fight with another student, James. The parent said that James had started the fight, and, of course, Tyson, was an "innocent" victim.

Since I am a sub, I don't know the children and their personalities very well. I had been in that classroom for only two days. But I do know what I saw.

I tried hard to calm the parent down, and, when she left, her tension had dissipated. But I was left with a bad feeling. I wrote a note to the classroom teacher about the incident.

Is there a better way to handle situations like this?

Samantha in Ocala, Florida

Dear Samantha,

Angry parents can be intimidating. As a sub, you are vulnerable because you don't know very much about the personalities of the children and you have no knowledge of the parents' idiosyncrasies. And yet, it's not uncommon to interact with parents. After all, you are their child's teacher for some period of time.

I have found that parents just want to be heard. My advice to you is to be a good listener. Use positive body language while listening. Eye contact is important. Let them talk and express their concerns. Act interested.

After the parent tells you her side of the story, express your thanks and indicate that her comments have given you more insight into the matter. You will readdress the issue, this time with more information and with another point of view. With her help, you now have a better handle on the situation. Don't promise any special outcome.

(continued)

Because parents often go to the top with complaints, be sure to be proactive and alert the classroom teacher and a school administrator. They will be thankful that you have given them a "heads-up."

You acted professionally within the scope of your job as a sub. Let the permanent professionals in the school resolve this delicate situation.

envelope or folder does exist, be sure to go through the following checklist before you depart.

- If the venue requires tickets or some other proof of advance payment, be certain to bring whatever is needed.
- If any children have special allergies, bring appropriate medications and be sure you understand what precautions you need to take. Consult with the nurse.
- Bring an emergency medical kit for cuts and scrapes.
- Bring a class roster and the name and telephone number of any contact person at the field trip venue.
- Be certain you have a name and contact number for the bus company. Ask if the driver has a cell phone number for you to call in case of emergency.

If you take the time to prepare, you'll be better able to handle any situation that might arise during the day.

Are name tags necessary?

Whether or not you decide to use name tags depends on the ages of the students, the venue for the field trip, and general school guidelines. For children in Kindergarten through Grade 6, name tags are a good idea for all trips, and they're essential when the students split up at an outdoor venue. For older children, name tags may not be as important because an older child can easily provide appropriate information if he or she is separated from the group.

Generally, the classroom teacher will have name tags prepared in advance for you. However, if name tags are not supplied, use a class roster as a guide for making them. Name tags can be pinned on or worn on a string around the neck. If you can get the self-adhesive name tags, use them. (Check in the office.) Put the name of the school on the name tag for better identification.

How do I manage the bus ride?

The bus ride to and from the field trip venue can be the most unpleasant part of the day. It's very important to review safety rules for the bus ride, such as staying in assigned seats and not putting hands or feet out the window. I always remind the students that the bus driver needs to concentrate on driving, and if he or she is distracted, no one is safe. I also tell students that I'll be taking notes on bus behavior and will give out rewards once we return to the classroom.

Some teachers play games or sing songs during the bus ride. This works well for a while; however, it's best to allow some relaxed "downtime" during the bus ride.

How do I keep track of the students?

Count the students on the bus (twice) before you depart. Prior to arrival, it's important to define certain times during the day (e.g., mid-morning, lunchtime, mid-afternoon, and, of course, departure at the end of the trip) when the entire class regroups at a prespecified location. The intent is to address any general problems, but more important, to take a head count.

Be certain that the parent chaperones realize that they should take their own group head counts on a regular basis. They should never allow students to wander without supervision.

What rules should I have the students follow?

The Utah State University has developed a *Substitute Teacher Handbook*[1] that provides a good set of rules for field trips:

Do:
Be courteous.
Stay with the group.
Listen attentively.
Follow safety regulations.

Don't:
Ask personal or irrelevant questions.
Lag behind.
Interrupt.
Take samples or touch unless given specific permission to
do so.

In addition to these simple rules, emphasize that students should keep track of the members of their group and immediately report any missing member to their chaperone or to you.

Summary

Most regular classroom teachers try hard to be present for a field trip, but sometimes an illness or a family emergency may intervene. That's when you get involved. Managing a student field trip well is just like anything else you do as a teacher—it takes preparation and effort. Try to apply the following guidelines:

• Be sure that children have signed permission slips. No
child will be allowed to depart without one.

---

1. Utah State University. *Substitute Teacher Handbook*. Available at sti.usu.edu.

- Check to ensure that you have all materials and information you'll need. Bring tickets and contact information. Take a first aid kit, and find out if any children have special allergies that may require medication.
- Make the best use of parent chaperones. Be sure that parent chaperones are aware of the rules and time to meet at the bus.
- Divide students into groups. Be sure to keep the most difficult students with you.
- Provide name tags. This is particularly important for younger children.
- Be sure to explain basic rules. The children must recognize that they represent the school and poor behavior will not be tolerated.
- Count heads. This is critically important and should be performed at the group level for the entire class before leaving, during the trip, and when leaving the trip to return to school.

A day away from the classroom is something that most students look forward to for weeks. To help make it an enjoyable experience for everyone involved, take the time to prepare as best you can and then manage the trip as it unfolds.

Appendix

Additional Resources for Subs

I've listed many of my favorite websites and books throughout *Substitute Teaching from A to Z*. However, many, many more useful resources are available, and I've created this Appendix to provide you with additional resource recommendations. These suggestions will broaden your knowledge of teaching, provide you with useful suggestions and hints, and inspire you in your quest for improvement. The website that accompanies this book, **substituteteachingatoz.com**, contains pointers to all of the resources noted in this appendix as well as pointers to many more useful sources.

Favorite Sources for Choosing Books

Some of the books recommended by these resources would make wonderful additions to your bag of tricks.

Scholastic Instructor Teachers' Picks
http://content.scholastic.com/browse/article.jsp?id=7817
Here you can find a list of the top fifty "teachers' picks." Many of the books are award-winning classics. This listing has been compiled by Scholastic and is presented in *Instructor* magazine. The article is divided into two sections,

top twenty-five picture books and top twenty-five chapter books.

American Library Association—Caldecott Medal Winners
ala.org/alsc/caldecott.html

The Caldecott Medal is given yearly to an artist of distinction for a picture book. The beautiful illustrations add a special dimension to the stories. This site lists all of the winners of the Caldecott Medal since 1938.

American Library Association—Newbery Medal Winners
ala.org/alsc/newbery.html

The Newbery Medal is given to an author for a distinguished contribution to children's literature. This website will point you to a list of Newbery winners from 1922 to the present.

A Children's Literature Web Guide
ucalgary.ca/~dKBrown/index.html

The University of Calgary provides pointers to book lists for children—divided into categories, such as the picture books, best literature for teens, highly recommended books for girls, and so on. This site contains resources for storytellers and commentary on children's books.

The Children's Book Council
cbcbooks.org

The Children's Book Council will keep you current on the latest releases in children's literature. The website showcases timely books, seasonal books, and more.

Teenreads
teenreads.com

This website gives you a listing of books specifically for teens, including books that were made into movies.

Young Adults Library Association
ala.org/ala/yalsa/booklistsawards/bestbooksya/
2000bestbooks.htm
This site is a wonderful resource for readings specifically for
young adults.

Inspirational Books About Teaching

No one ever said that teaching is easy, and even the very best
teachers need inspiration once in a while. The books listed
in this section are inspiring for teachers and for anyone who
wants to understand teachers.

Liesveld, R., J. Miller, and J. Robison. *Teach with Your
Strengths: How Great Teachers Inspire Their Students.*
Gallup Press, 2005.
Based on research, this book teaches you how to use your
strengths to become a good teacher.

Clark, R. *The Essential 55.* **Hyperion, 2004.**
From the heart, author Ron Clark details his experiences as
a successful teacher. His stories will inspire you.

McCourt, F. *Teacher Man: A Memoir.* **Scribner, 2005.**
The author of the national bestseller *Angela's Ashes*, Frank
McCourt, tells of his early years as a substitute teacher and
then as a regular high school teacher in New York City. He
made some mistakes but stumbled on success. His lessons
will encourage you to improve.

Done, P. *32 Third Graders and One Class Bunny: Life Lessons from Teaching.* **Gallup Press, 2005.**
I know you'll enjoy this beautiful and very funny book of
essays about Phillip Done's experience teaching third graders. He writes in a style that makes it seem as if he is speaking directly to you while you're both eating the cafeteria
lunch together!

Katz, R. *Elaine's Circle: A Teacher, a Student, a Classroom and One Unforgettable Year.* Marlowe & Co., 2005.
This is the story of a teacher who makes a difference in a child's life. A student is diagnosed with a brain tumor, and his teacher decides that if the child cannot come to class, why not have the class come to him. Inspiring!

Codell, E. *Educating Esme: Diary of a Teacher's First Year.* Algonquin Books, 2001.
This is a diary of a new, idealistic teacher in the Chicago city schools.

Classroom Management Resources

As I've emphasized throughout this book, classroom management is a skill that can be learned. The books listed in this section will provide you with invaluable guidance.

Canter, L. *Assertive Discipline.* Canter and Associates, 2001.
Lee Canter, a well-respected teaching guru, gives practical advice on behavior management.

Nelsen, J. *Positive Discipline.* Three Rivers Press, 2001.
Problem-solving techniques and class meetings are the focus of this guide.

Wong, H., and R. Wong. *The First Days of School.* Harry Wong Publications, 2004.
Harry and Rosemary Wong's book can be found in virtually every school's library. The chapter on classroom management emphasizes positive expectations, rules, and a good discipline plan.

Evertson, C., E. Emmer, and M. Worsham. *Classroom Management for Elementary Teachers* (7th ed.). Allyn & Bacon, 2005.
This book outlines procedures and routines in a specific, practical manner.

Rubinstein, G. *Reluctant Disciplinarian: Advice on Class-room Management from a Softy Who Became (Eventually) a Successful Teacher.* Cottonwood Press, 1999.
Useful and informative, this book includes real-life case studies for examples.

Springer, S., B. Alexander, and K. Persiani-Becker. *The Organized Teacher.* The McGraw-Hill Companies, Inc., 2005.
This book is full of ideas for classroom management and behavior management. You'll find many classroom incentives and rewards for those days when you need something extra. Make copies for your Bag of Tricks.

Springer, S., B. Alexander, and K. Persiani-Becker. *The Creative Teacher.* The McGraw-Hill Companies, Inc., 2007.
In the second book by this creative team, you'll find ready-to-use materials and reproducibles, templates, art projects, and helpful hints.

If you need a quick fix for a classroom management problem, one of the following websites may be helpful:

The Really Best List of Classroom Management Resources
http://drwilliampmartin.tripod.com/reallybest.htm
Discover ways of catching kids "being good," a very effective method for classroom management, from sticker charts to the raffle ticket system. Practical solutions that work!

Eliminate Disruptive Behavior
adhdsolution.com/teachers
You will find a discussion of ways of reaching the ADHD students that you will find in every class.

ProTeacher Community

proteacher.com/030001.shtml

Real teachers (not academics) give advice on classroom management. You will find ideas such as coupons, tickets, behavior charts, and so on.

Resource Guide to Bullying

state.sc.us/dmh/schoolbased/bullying.htm

If you've encountered bullying in the classroom and need help in managing the situation, the links at this site will provide guidance.

Ideas for Teaching—All Subject Areas

Some teaching resources are difficult to categorize, yet provide useful information for a sub. The listings that follow cover a variety of teaching topics.

Teachnology—Online Teacher Resources

teach-nology.com

Lesson plans, printable worksheets, games, rubrics, and quality worksheets can be found at this site.

Teaching Ideas Center

ncte.org/profdev/online/ideas

Language arts ideas are provided by the National Council of Teachers of English.

Ed Helper

edhelper.com

Here you can find worksheets to thematic units across all areas of the curriculum, from pre-Kindergarten to high school.

Scholastic
teacher.scholastic.com/lessonplans
Well-respected publisher Scholastic provides lesson plans for teachers in an organized fashion. The site also includes book clubs, message boards, and so on.

Lesson Plans Page.Com
lessonplanspage.com
This site features seasonal lesson plans, including health, PE, art, language arts, and math.

Federal Resources for Educational Excellence
free.ed.gov/index.cfm
Teaching resources from federal agencies can be found here, including maps and time lines as well as resources related to art and music.

TeacherNet
teachernet.gov.uk/teachingandlearning/resource materials
This site provides community links and addresses a variety of global issues and school issues.

Index

Note: Entries in *italics* refer to titles of books or websites.

About the Author

Barbara L. Pressman has more than thirty years of teaching experience as a classroom teacher and as a tutor in New Jersey, Connecticut, and Florida.

Currently, Barbara is an adjunct professor in the College of Education at Florida Atlantic University (FAU) where she serves as a university supervisor of student teachers in the Palm Beach County school district. In addition, she is one of the founding participants and Master Mentor in an innovative new FAU program that trains education majors to sub and assist in local schools. The program's goal is to supply qualified, trained subs to local schools using a combination of mentoring and training. University students improve their teaching skills using real-life experience. Many of the ideas contained in *Substitute Teaching from A to Z* are being applied daily as part of the FAU program.

Barbara has a B.S. and M.S. in Elementary Education from the University of Bridgeport. She has two grown sons who work in media related fields. She lives with her husband Roger Pressman in South Florida.